WEB DEVELOPMENT UNLEASHED

A Practical Guide for Beginners

Kiet Huynh

Table of Contents

Introduction 5

  About This Book 5

  Who Is This Book For? 9

  How to Use This Book 13

  Web Development: An Overview 17

CHAPTER I: Getting Started with Web Development 22

  1.1 The World of Web Development 22

  1.2 HTML: The Foundation of the Web 26

  1.3 Setting Up Your Development Environment 32

  1.4 Your First HTML Page 36

  1.5 Understanding the DOM (Document Object Model) 40

  1.6 Basic HTML Elements 45

CHAPTER II: Styling Your Web Pages with CSS 50

  2.1 Introduction to Cascading Style Sheets (CSS) 50

  2.2 Selectors and Styles 55

  2.3 CSS Properties and Values 61

  2.4 Adding Styles to HTML Elements 66

  2.5 Creating Layouts with CSS 70

  2.6 CSS Box Model 74

CHAPTER III: JavaScript Essentials 77

  3.1 Introduction to JavaScript 77

  3.2 Variables and Data Types 81

  3.3 Operators and Expressions 84

  3.4 Control Structures: Conditional Statements and Loops 87

  3.5 Functions and Scope 92

  3.6 Handling Events and User Interactions 95

CHAPTER IV: Building Interactive Web Pages **98**

4.1 DOM Manipulation with JavaScript 98

4.2 Event Handling and Event Listeners 101

4.3 Creating Dynamic Content 104

4.4 Form Validation and User Feedback 107

4.5 Working with Images and Media 110

CHAPTER V: Responsive Web Design **114**

5.1 The Importance of Responsive Design 114

5.2 CSS Media Queries 117

5.3 Flexible Layouts with Flexbox 121

5.4 Creating Responsive Navigation Menus 124

5.5 Optimizing for Mobile Devices 128

CHAPTER VI: Web Development Tools **131**

6.1 Code Editors and Integrated Development Environments (IDEs) 131

6.2 Browser Developer Tools 134

6.3 Version Control with Git and GitHub 137

6.4 Web Development Extensions and Plugins 141

CHAPTER VII: Putting It All Together: Practical Projects **144**

7.1 Project 1: Personal Portfolio Website 144

7.2 Project 2: Interactive Photo Gallery 148

7.3 Project 3: Contact Form with Server-Side Integration 152

CHAPTER VIII: Web Hosting and Deployment **156**

8.1 Choosing a Domain Name 156

8.2 Selecting a Web Hosting Provider 159

8.3 Uploading Your Website 162

8.4 Testing and Troubleshooting 165

8.5 Launching Your Website 169

CHAPTER IX: Web Development Best Practices **173**

9.1 Writing Clean and Maintainable Code 173

9.2 Performance Optimization 177

9.3 Web Security Basics 181

9.4 Accessibility Guidelines 185

9.5 Keeping Up with Web Development Trends 189

CHAPTER X: Beyond the Basics: What's Next? **193**

10.1 Exploring Advanced JavaScript and Frameworks 193

10.2 Backend Development and Server-Side Programming 197

10.3 Database Integration 201

10.4 Building Web Applications 205

10.5 A Glimpse into the Future of Web Development 210

Appendix A   HTML and CSS Reference **214**

A.1 HTML Elements and Attributes 214

A.2 Common CSS Properties and Values 216

Appendix B   JavaScript Reference **219**

B.1 JavaScript Objects and Methods 219

B.2 Common JavaScript Events 221

Glossary **226**

Key Terms and Definitions 226

Conclusion **229**

Introduction

About This Book

Welcome to "Web Development Unleashed: A Practical Guide for Beginners." In this section, we will provide a detailed exploration of what makes this book unique and how it's structured to empower you with the skills and knowledge needed to become a proficient web developer.

Why This Book Matters

Web development is the backbone of our digital age, driving everything from personal blogs to global e-commerce platforms and interactive web applications. Understanding how websites are created and maintained has never been more relevant or empowering. This book aims to demystify web development and make it accessible to everyone, regardless of their prior experience.

What Sets This Book Apart

Web Development Unleashed stands out for several key reasons:

1. Comprehensive Learning Path: This book provides a comprehensive and systematic learning path. We begin with the absolute basics and progress to more advanced topics, ensuring that you have a solid foundation to build upon.

2. Practical Focus: We believe in learning by doing. Throughout this book, you'll find practical exercises, real-world examples, and hands-on projects that allow you to apply what you've learned in a meaningful way.

3. Beginner-Friendly Approach: No prior coding experience is assumed. We use plain language, provide clear explanations, and avoid unnecessary technical jargon to make web development concepts accessible to everyone.

4. Structured Content: Each chapter builds on the knowledge gained in the previous one. This logical progression ensures that you grasp fundamental concepts before moving on to more advanced material.

5. Real-World Relevance: The skills you'll acquire here are directly applicable to real-life situations. Whether you're looking to launch your website, pursue a career in web development, or simply gain a deeper understanding of the digital world, this book equips you with practical knowledge.

6. Clear and Concise: We believe that clarity is essential. Concepts are explained in a straightforward manner, and we provide numerous examples to illustrate each idea, helping you grasp even the most complex topics.

7. Abundance of Resources: Learning web development is an ongoing journey. In addition to the content in this book, we guide you to further resources, online tutorials, and tools that can enhance your learning and keep you up-to-date with the latest developments in web development.

Who Can Benefit From This Book

Web Development Unleashed is designed for a diverse audience:

- Complete Beginners: If you're entirely new to web development, this book is your starting point. We assume no prior knowledge and guide you through the fundamentals.

- **Students:** Whether you're studying web development academically or as a personal interest, this book offers a structured and practical approach to learning.

- **Entrepreneurs and Small Business Owners**: Understanding web development can be a game-changer for managing your online presence and collaborating effectively with web developers.

- **Curious Minds:** If you're curious about how websites work and want to experiment with creating your own, this book provides a welcoming introduction.

What You'll Learn

Within the pages of *Web Development Unleashed,* you'll embark on a journey that covers a wide range of essential topics:

1. Foundations of Web Development: We'll start at the very beginning, introducing you to the core concepts and technologies that underpin the web.

2. HTML and CSS Mastery: You'll become proficient in HTML for structuring web content and CSS for styling and layout.

3. JavaScript Essentials: Dive into JavaScript, the language that adds interactivity and dynamic behavior to web pages.

4. Building Responsive Websites: Learn how to create websites that adapt gracefully to various screen sizes and devices.

5. Web Development Tools: Discover the essential tools, code editors, and development environments that streamline your workflow.

6. Practical Projects: Apply your newly acquired skills to real-world projects, from creating your personal portfolio to developing interactive web elements.

7. Web Hosting and Deployment: Take your web creations live, from selecting a domain name to deploying your websites for global access.

8. Web Development Best Practices: Master coding practices, optimize website performance, enhance web security, and ensure accessibility for all users.

9. Beyond the Basics: Explore advanced topics, including JavaScript frameworks, backend development, and the creation of web applications.

Who Is This Book For?

This book has been meticulously crafted to cater to a diverse audience with varying levels of familiarity with web development. Whether you're an absolute beginner or have some prior experience, here's a detailed breakdown of who can benefit from *Web Development Unleashed:*

1. Complete Beginners: This book is your ideal starting point if you have zero prior knowledge of web development. We assume no familiarity with coding or web technologies. If you've ever wondered how websites are created and want to learn from scratch, you're in the right place.

2. Students: Whether you're a high school or college student pursuing a degree related to web development or computer science, this book complements your coursework. It provides a practical, hands-on approach that reinforces academic learning.

3. Career Changers: If you're considering a career shift into the world of technology and web development, this book offers a structured path to acquiring the foundational skills needed to embark on this exciting journey.

4. Small Business Owners and Entrepreneurs: As a business owner, understanding the basics of web development can be invaluable. It enables you to manage your online presence, communicate effectively with web developers, and make informed decisions about your digital strategies.

5. Curious Individuals: You don't need a specific reason to explore web development. If you're simply curious about how websites work, enjoy problem-solving, or want to experiment with building your own web projects, this book provides an accessible entry point.

6. Hobbyists and Bloggers: If you're a hobbyist looking to enhance your personal blog or website, this book equips you with the skills to make your online presence more dynamic and engaging.

7. Professionals in Related Fields: Professionals in fields like graphic design, digital marketing, or content creation can benefit from understanding web development. It allows you to better collaborate with developers and gain a deeper appreciation of the web technologies that shape your work.

8. Self-Learners and Lifelong Learners: Learning web development is not restricted by age or background. If you have a passion for continuous learning and personal growth, this book provides a structured path to acquire valuable skills.

Specific Scenarios

Let's explore a few specific scenarios to illustrate how this book can address the unique needs of different individuals:

- **Scenario 1 - Sarah, the High School Student:** Sarah is a high school student interested in computers and technology. She's curious about web development but has no prior coding experience. Web Development Unleashed provides Sarah with a beginner-friendly introduction, gradually building her skills from the ground up. By the end of the book, Sarah will have the confidence to create her own web projects and might even consider pursuing web development as a career.

- **Scenario 2 - David, the Small Business Owner:** David owns a local bakery and wants to establish an online presence to reach a wider customer base. He's not tech-savvy but wants to understand the basics of web development to effectively communicate with a web designer. This book provides David with the knowledge he needs to make informed decisions about his website's design and functionality.

- **Scenario 3 - Emily, the Career Changer:** Emily is working in a field unrelated to technology but has a strong desire to transition into web development. She's seeking a structured learning path that covers all the essential skills. **Web Development Unleashed** offers Emily a clear roadmap to acquiring the foundational knowledge and practical experience necessary for a career switch.

How to Tailor Your Learning Experience

To maximize the benefits of this book, consider the following strategies based on your specific situation:

1. Beginners: Start from Chapter 1 and progress sequentially. Complete the exercises and projects to reinforce your learning.

2. Students: Supplement your academic coursework with the practical insights and projects provided in this book. Apply what you learn to class assignments.

3. Career Changers: Approach this book with a career-oriented mindset. Use it to build a strong foundation in web development and consider additional specialized courses or certifications for your desired career path.

4. Small Business Owners: Focus on chapters related to web design, user experience, and web hosting. This knowledge will empower you to make informed decisions about your business website.

5. Curious Individuals: Feel free to explore the book at your own pace. Focus on the areas that pique your interest, and don't hesitate to experiment with your web projects.

6. Hobbyists and Bloggers: Enhance your website by applying the styling and interactivity techniques covered in this book. Experiment with creating dynamic content to engage your audience.

7. Professionals in Related Fields: Gain insights into web development to improve collaboration with developers and enhance your digital marketing, design, or content creation skills.

8. Self-Learners and Lifelong Learners: Embrace web development as a lifelong learning journey. Use this book as a stepping stone to more advanced topics and specialized areas within web development.

In conclusion, **Web Development Unleashed: A Practical Guide for Beginners** is a versatile resource that caters to a wide range of learners and professionals. It provides the foundational knowledge and practical skills needed to excel in the ever-evolving field of web development. Whether you're pursuing a career, exploring a new hobby, or enhancing your digital literacy, this book is your trusted companion on your web development journey.

How to Use This Book

In this section, we'll dive into practical strategies on how to make the most of Web Development Unleashed: A Practical Guide for Beginners. We understand that effective learning requires structure and guidance, so we'll provide a step-by-step approach to using this book to its fullest potential.

1. Sequential Learning Path

This book is structured to build your web development skills progressively. We recommend following this sequential learning path for the best results:

- **Begin at the Beginning:** Start with Chapter 1, "Getting Started with Web Development." This chapter introduces you to the foundational concepts of web development and sets the stage for your learning journey.

- **Read Actively:** As you read, be an active learner. Take notes, underline key points, and jot down questions you have. Engaging with the material actively helps with retention.

- **Complete Exercises:** Each chapter includes exercises designed to reinforce your understanding. These exercises are hands-on opportunities to apply what you've learned. Don't skip them! The more you practice, the more confident you'll become.

- **Work on Projects:** Practical projects are scattered throughout the book. These are valuable opportunities to build real web content. Take the time to work on these projects; they provide a taste of what real web development entails.

- **Review and Reflect:** After completing a chapter, take a moment to review what you've learned. Reflect on how the new knowledge fits into the bigger picture of web development.

2. Hands-On Practice

Web development is a skill that is best learned through practice. Here's how to incorporate hands-on practice into your learning:

- **Code Along:** As you read, open your code editor and type out the code examples in the book. Don't just read the code; understand it and run it on your machine.

- **Experiment:** Don't be afraid to experiment with the code. Modify it, break it, and see what happens. This type of exploration can deepen your understanding.

- **Create Personal Projects:** In addition to the book's projects, consider working on personal projects that align with your interests. It could be a blog, a hobby website, or anything that excites you. Apply the concepts you've learned to your projects.

3. Seek Clarification

Don't hesitate to seek clarification when you encounter concepts or problems that are unclear. Here's how:

- **Use Online Resources:** If you're stuck on a particular topic, turn to online resources like Stack Overflow, developer forums, or YouTube tutorials. These resources often provide practical solutions to common challenges.

- **Reach Out for Help:** If you're part of a learning community or taking a course, don't hesitate to ask questions and seek guidance from instructors or fellow learners.

4. Additional Resources

Throughout the book, you'll find references to additional resources, including websites, tutorials, and tools. Take advantage of these references to deepen your knowledge:

- **Online Tutorials**: Many web development concepts have dedicated online tutorials that provide in-depth explanations and examples. Explore these tutorials to reinforce your understanding.

- **Documentation:** Familiarize yourself with official documentation for web technologies like HTML, CSS, and JavaScript. Documentation is a valuable resource for learning and reference.

- **Development Tools**: Experiment with various code editors and development tools. Find the ones that suit your preferences and workflow.

5. Set Goals

Setting clear goals can help you stay motivated and focused. Here's how to set effective learning goals:

- **Short-Term Goals:** Define what you want to accomplish after each chapter or project. For example, your goal after a CSS chapter might be to create a basic webpage with custom styling.

- **Long-Term Goals:** Consider your broader objectives. Do you want to build a portfolio website, contribute to an open-source project, or pursue a career in web development? Setting long-term goals will give your learning purpose.

6. Don't Rush

Learning web development is a journey, not a race. Take your time to understand each concept fully before moving on to the next. Mastery requires patience and persistence.

7. Embrace Challenges

Challenges and problem-solving are integral to web development. Don't be discouraged by errors or roadblocks; instead, view them as opportunities to learn and grow.

8. Collaborate and Share

Consider collaborating with fellow learners or joining web development communities. Sharing your knowledge and experiences can enhance your understanding and provide valuable insights.

In conclusion, **Web Development Unleashed: A Practical Guide for Beginners** is a resource designed to empower you with web development skills. To make the most of this book, follow the structured learning path, practice actively, seek clarification when needed, and set goals that align with your aspirations. Remember that web development is both an art and a science, and your journey should be enjoyable as you unlock the possibilities of the digital world.

Web Development: An Overview

In this section, we embark on a comprehensive journey through the fascinating realm of web development. We'll explore the core concepts, technologies, and processes that underpin the creation of websites and web applications. By the end of this overview, you'll have a clear understanding of what web development entails and its significance in today's digital landscape.

The Web Development Ecosystem

Imagine the internet as a vast digital universe, and websites as the stars within it. Web development is the craft of creating and maintaining these stars, making them shine brightly, and ensuring they function seamlessly. To navigate this universe effectively, let's break down the web development ecosystem into its key components:

1. Frontend Development: Frontend developers are like architects and interior designers of the web. They focus on the user interface (UI) and user experience (UX) aspects of websites. This includes designing web pages, creating layouts, and enhancing interactivity using technologies like HTML, CSS, and JavaScript.

Example: When you visit an e-commerce website and browse products, add items to your cart, or apply filters, you're interacting with the frontend.

2. Backend Development: Backend developers are the engineers behind the scenes. They build the server-side infrastructure that powers websites. This includes handling user data, managing databases, and ensuring security and scalability.

Example: When you log in to a social media platform, the backend authenticates your credentials, retrieves your data from the database, and serves it to the frontend.

3. Full Stack Development: Full stack developers are versatile professionals who work on both the frontend and backend. They have a holistic understanding of web development, allowing them to build entire web applications from start to finish.

Example: Full stack developers can create a complete e-commerce website, handling everything from the product catalog (frontend) to the payment processing (backend).

4. Web Technologies: The web relies on a rich set of technologies and standards. HTML (Hypertext Markup Language) defines the structure of web content, CSS (Cascading Style Sheets) controls its appearance, and JavaScript adds interactivity. Other technologies like PHP, Python, Ruby, and Java are used on the backend.

Example: HTML tags define headings, paragraphs, images, and links on a web page. CSS styles determine colors, fonts, and layout, while JavaScript enables dynamic behavior like form validation.

5. Web Browsers: Web browsers are the gateways to the internet. Popular browsers like Chrome, Firefox, Safari, and Edge render web content and execute JavaScript. Developers must ensure their websites work smoothly across various browsers.

Example: When you enter a website's URL in your browser, it retrieves and displays the web content, applying styles and running scripts as needed.

The Web Development Process

Creating a website or web application is a structured process that involves multiple stages. Let's outline the typical steps in the web development journey:

1. Planning: The first step is defining the project's goals, target audience, and features. This stage includes creating wireframes and mockups to visualize the website's layout and functionality.

Example: A planning stage for an e-learning platform might involve outlining user roles (students, instructors), defining course structures, and sketching the user interface.

2. Design: Designers craft the website's visual identity during this phase. They select color schemes, typography, and create designs that align with the project's goals and branding.

Example: A designer might create a sleek and user-friendly design for an online magazine, considering factors like readability and aesthetics.

3. Development: Developers bring designs to life using web technologies. Frontend developers write HTML, CSS, and JavaScript to create responsive and interactive web pages. Backend developers build server logic and databases to support the application.

Example: During development, a team of developers could build the frontend for an e-commerce website to display products and enable customers to make purchases.

4. Testing: Quality assurance is essential to ensure the website functions correctly and is free of bugs and errors. Testing involves various levels, including unit testing, integration testing, and user acceptance testing (UAT).

Example: Testers may verify that the payment processing functionality on an online marketplace works smoothly and securely.

5. Deployment: Once thoroughly tested, the website is deployed to a web server and made accessible to the public. This may involve setting up domain names and configuring web hosting services.

Example: After development and testing, an educational institution's website is deployed to a web server, allowing students to access course materials online.

6. Maintenance: Websites require ongoing maintenance to keep them secure and up to date. This includes regular software updates, security patches, and content updates.

Example: The maintenance phase ensures that an online news portal remains responsive and secure, even as new articles are published.

The Impact of Web Development

Web development has a profound impact on our daily lives and the broader digital landscape:

- **Economic Growth**: Web development drives e-commerce, online services, and digital marketing, contributing significantly to global economic growth.

- **Information Access:** It democratizes access to information, enabling people worldwide to learn, connect, and access resources.

- **Innovation:** Web development fuels innovation, leading to the creation of new technologies and business models.

- **Global Connectivity:** The web connects people, businesses, and cultures across the globe, fostering collaboration and understanding.

In conclusion, web development is a dynamic and multidimensional field that encompasses frontend and backend development, a wide array of technologies, and a structured development process. It plays a pivotal role in shaping the digital world we interact with daily. As we delve deeper into this book, you'll gain hands-on experience and insights into the exciting world of web development, equipping you with the skills to create and innovate in the digital age.

CHAPTER I
Getting Started with Web Development

1.1 The World of Web Development

In this section, we'll embark on our web development journey by diving into the fascinating world of web development. You'll gain a solid understanding of what web development is, its history, and the role it plays in the digital age.

What is Web Development?

At its core, web development is the art and science of building and maintaining websites and web applications. It involves creating web pages, designing their layout and appearance, adding interactivity, and ensuring they function correctly. In essence, web developers are the architects, builders, and custodians of the digital realm we interact with daily.

A Brief History of the Web

Before we delve deeper, let's take a quick trip down memory lane to understand how the web has evolved:

- **Early Days (1990s):** The web's inception is credited to Sir Tim Berners-Lee, who developed the World Wide Web (WWW) in 1990. Early websites were simple and text-based, primarily used for sharing information.

- The Dot-com Boom (Late 1990s): The late '90s saw the emergence of e-commerce giants like Amazon and eBay, sparking the dot-com boom. Websites became more dynamic and interactive.

- Web 2.0 (Early 2000s): This era marked the rise of user-generated content and social media. Websites like Facebook and YouTube allowed users to create and share content.

- Mobile Revolution (Late 2000s): With the advent of smartphones, web development shifted towards creating mobile-responsive websites and applications.

- The Modern Web (Present): Today's web is a complex ecosystem of websites, web apps, progressive web apps (PWAs), and single-page applications (SPAs). It's characterized by rich interactivity, multimedia content, and a focus on user experience.

Roles in Web Development

Web development encompasses various roles, each with its own responsibilities:

- Frontend Developer: Frontend developers focus on the visual aspects of websites. They use HTML, CSS, and JavaScript to create web pages, design layouts, and add interactivity.

- Backend Developer: Backend developers work behind the scenes, managing servers, databases, and the logic that powers web applications. They ensure data is securely stored and retrieved.

- Full Stack Developer: Full stack developers are proficient in both frontend and backend development. They have a holistic understanding of web development.

Importance of Web Development

Web development is pivotal in today's digital landscape for several reasons:

- **Digital Presence:** Websites are the digital storefronts of businesses, enabling them to reach a global audience 24/7.

- **E-Commerce:** The web facilitates online shopping, driving the growth of e-commerce businesses.

- **Information Access:** It democratizes access to information, education, and resources.

- **Innovation:** Web development fuels innovation, leading to new technologies and digital solutions.

- **Global Connectivity:** The web connects people, fostering collaboration and communication across the globe.

Web Development Technologies

To get started with web development, it's essential to understand some fundamental technologies:

- **HTML (Hypertext Markup Language):** HTML is the backbone of web pages. It defines the structure and content of a web page using elements like headings, paragraphs, lists, and links.

- **CSS (Cascading Style Sheets):** CSS is responsible for the presentation and styling of web pages. It controls colors, fonts, layout, and design.

- **JavaScript:** JavaScript is a programming language that adds interactivity to web pages. It enables dynamic behavior like form validation, animations, and real-time updates.

Getting Ready to Dive In

As we progress through this book, you'll gain hands-on experience with these technologies and embark on practical projects that will reinforce your understanding. Our journey begins with HTML, the foundation of the web, in the next section.

Before we start coding, it's essential to set up your development environment. In section 1.3, we'll guide you through the process step by step.

By the end of this chapter, you'll have a solid grasp of the web development landscape, its history, and the technologies that power it. You'll be well-prepared to embark on your hands-on web development journey. So, let's dive in and explore the exciting world of web development!

1.2 HTML: The Foundation of the Web

In this section, we will explore HTML (Hypertext Markup Language), which serves as the cornerstone of web development. HTML is the language used to structure web content, define its elements, and create the foundation of every web page you encounter.

Understanding HTML

HTML is a markup language that uses tags to structure content on a web page. These tags tell web browsers how to display different elements, such as headings, paragraphs, images, and links. Let's break down the basics:

- **Tags:** HTML tags are enclosed in angle brackets, like `<tagname>`. They come in pairs—an opening tag and a closing tag. The closing tag has a forward slash before the tag name, like `</tagname>`. For example, `<p>` is an opening tag for a paragraph, and `</p>` is the corresponding closing tag.

- **Elements:** Elements are created by placing content between opening and closing tags. For instance, to create a paragraph, you'd use `<p>` to open it and `</p>` to close it, with the paragraph text in between.

HTML Document Structure

An HTML document typically follows this structure:

```html
<!DOCTYPE html>
<html>
```

```
  <head>
    <meta charset="UTF-8">
    <title>Page Title</title>
  </head>
  <body>
    <h1>This is a Heading</h1>
    <p>This is a paragraph.</p>
    <img src="image.jpg" alt="An image">
    <a href="https://www.example.com">Visit Example.com</a>
  </body>
</html>
```

- `<!DOCTYPE html>`: This declaration tells the browser that the document is written in HTML5, the latest version of HTML.

- `<html>`: The root element that wraps all other elements on the page.

- `<head>`: Contains meta-information about the document, such as character encoding and the page title (displayed in the browser's title bar or tab).

- `<body>`: The main content of the web page, including headings, paragraphs, images, and links.

Common HTML Elements

Let's explore some essential HTML elements that you'll frequently use:

1. `<h1>, <h2>, <h3>, ... <h6>`: Headings provide structure to your content, with `<h1>` being the highest level (main heading) and `<h6>` the lowest.

```html
<h1>Main Heading</h1>
<h2>Subheading 1</h2>
<h2>Subheading 2</h2>
```

2. `<p>`: Paragraphs are used for text content.

```html
<p>This is a paragraph of text.</p>
```

3. `<a>`: Anchor tags create hyperlinks to other web pages or resources.

```html
<a href="https://www.example.com">Visit Example.com</a>
```

4. `<img>`: Image tags display images on your web page.

```html
<img src="image.jpg" alt="An image">
```

5. `<ul>` and `<ol>`: Unordered lists (`<ul>`) create bulleted lists, while ordered lists (`<ol>`) create numbered lists. List items are defined using `<li>`.

```html
<ul>
  <li>Item 1</li>
  <li>Item 2</li>
  <li>Item 3</li>
</ul>
```

6. `<div>`: The division element is a container for grouping other elements. It's often used for layout and styling purposes.

```html
<div class="container">
  <p>Content inside a div.</p>
</div>
```

HTML Attributes

HTML tags can have attributes that provide additional information or properties. Attributes are added to the opening tag and are specified as name-value pairs. For example:

```html
<a href="https://www.example.com" title="Visit Example.com">Example</a>
```

In this example, `href` is an attribute that specifies the link's destination, and `title` is an attribute that provides a tooltip when the user hovers over the link.

Practical Example

Let's create a simple HTML document together. Open a text editor and follow these steps:

1. Create a new file and save it with an `.html` extension, such as `index.html`.

2. Add the basic structure of an HTML document:

```html
<!DOCTYPE html>
<html>
  <head>
    <meta charset="UTF-8">
    <title>My First HTML Page</title>
```

```
  </head>
  <body>
    <h1>Welcome to My Web Page</h1>
    <p>This is a paragraph of text.</p>
  </body>
</html>
```

3. Save the file and open it in a web browser. You should see your first HTML page with a heading and a paragraph.

Congratulations! You've just created and viewed your first HTML page.

HTML serves as the foundation for web development. Understanding its structure, elements, and attributes is a crucial step in your journey. In the next section, we'll explore how to set up your development environment, so you can start building web pages and applications with ease.

1.3 Setting Up Your Development Environment

In this section, we will guide you through setting up your development environment for web development. Having the right tools and software in place is crucial to create, test, and deploy web applications effectively.

Choose a Text Editor or Integrated Development Environment (IDE)

The first step in setting up your web development environment is selecting a text editor or an integrated development environment (IDE). These tools are where you'll write your HTML, CSS, and JavaScript code. Here are some popular options:

1. Visual Studio Code (VSCode): VSCode is a free, open-source code editor developed by Microsoft. It's highly extensible and has a vast library of extensions that can enhance your web development workflow.

2. Sublime Text: Sublime Text is known for its speed and simplicity. It's a lightweight text editor with a clean interface and a rich set of features.

3. Atom: Atom is an open-source text editor developed by GitHub. It's highly customizable and has a vibrant community creating packages and themes.

4. WebStorm: If you prefer a full-featured IDE, WebStorm is a popular choice. It's designed specifically for web development and includes powerful coding and debugging features.

Choose the one that suits your preferences and install it on your computer.

Install a Web Browser

Web browsers are essential tools for web development because they allow you to preview and test your web pages. While you likely already have a web browser installed, it's a good idea to have multiple browsers for testing purposes. Some popular options include:

1. Google Chrome: Known for its developer-friendly tools, Chrome is a popular choice among web developers.

2. Mozilla Firefox: Firefox offers a developer edition with built-in developer tools, making it a great option for testing.

3. Microsoft Edge: Edge is another browser that comes with developer tools and is useful for testing on Windows machines.

Set Up Version Control

Version control is crucial for tracking changes in your code, collaborating with others, and rolling back to previous versions if needed. Git is the most widely used version control system, and GitHub provides a platform for hosting and sharing your code.

Here's how to set up Git and GitHub:

1. Install Git: Download and install Git from the official website (https://git-scm.com/). Follow the installation instructions for your operating system.

2. Create a GitHub Account: If you don't have one already, sign up for a GitHub account (https://github.com/).

3. Configure Git: Open a terminal or command prompt and set your Git username and email:

```
git config --global user.name "Your Name"
git config --global user.email "your.email@example.com"
```

4. Connect Git to GitHub: You can authenticate your Git client with GitHub using SSH keys or personal access tokens. GitHub provides clear instructions on setting up authentication in your account settings.

Install Node.js and npm (Node Package Manager)

Node.js is a JavaScript runtime that allows you to run JavaScript on the server side. npm is a package manager that lets you install and manage libraries and tools for your web development projects.

Here's how to install Node.js and npm:

1. Download Node.js: Visit the official Node.js website (https://nodejs.org/) and download the LTS (Long-Term Support) version for your operating system. LTS versions are recommended for stability.

2. Install Node.js: Run the downloaded installer and follow the installation instructions.

3. Verify Installation: Open a terminal or command prompt and run the following commands to verify that Node.js and npm are installed:

```
node -v
npm -v
```

You should see the version numbers displayed, indicating a successful installation.

Conclusion

With your development environment set up, you're ready to start building web applications. You have chosen a text editor or IDE, installed web browsers for testing, set up version control with Git and GitHub, and installed Node.js and npm.

In the next section, "1.4 Your First HTML Page," we will put your development environment to use by creating your first HTML page. You'll learn how to structure HTML documents and create content within them. Get ready to start your hands-on journey into web development!

1.4 Your First HTML Page

In this section, we will walk you through the process of creating your very first HTML page. You'll learn the basic structure of an HTML document, how to add content, and view your web page in a browser.

HTML Document Structure

Before diving into creating your HTML page, let's understand the fundamental structure of an HTML document. Every HTML document consists of the following elements:

```html
<!DOCTYPE html>
<html>
  <head>
    <meta charset="UTF-8">
    <title>Your Page Title</title>
  </head>
  <body>
    <!-- Your content goes here -->
  </body>
</html>
```

- `<!DOCTYPE html>`: This declaration tells the browser that you're using HTML5, the latest version of HTML.

- `<html>`: The root element that wraps all other elements in your document.

- `<head>`: This section contains meta-information about your document, such as character encoding and the page title.

- `<meta charset="UTF-8">`: Specifies the character encoding for your document. UTF-8 is a widely used encoding that supports various characters and languages.

- `<title>`: Sets the title of your web page, which appears in the browser's title bar or tab.

- `<body>`: The main content of your web page goes here.

Creating Your First HTML Page

Let's create a simple HTML page together. Follow these steps:

1. Choose a Text Editor: Open the text editor or IDE you selected in the previous section (e.g., Visual Studio Code, Sublime Text).

2. Create a New File: Create a new file and save it with an `.html` extension, such as `index.html`.

3. Basic HTML Structure: Start by creating the basic structure of an HTML document. You can copy and paste the following code:

```html
```

```html
<!DOCTYPE html>
<html>
 <head>
  <meta charset="UTF-8">
  <title>My First HTML Page</title>
 </head>
 <body>
  <h1>Hello, World!</h1>
  <p>This is my first HTML page.</p>
 </body>
</html>
```

4. Add Content: In the `<body>` section, you can add content using HTML elements. Here, we have added a heading (`<h1>`) and a paragraph (`<p>`). You can replace the content with anything you like.

5. Save the File: Save the file after adding your content.

6. View in a Web Browser: To view your HTML page, simply open the file in a web browser. You can either double-click the file or right-click and choose "Open with" your preferred browser. Your web page will display, and you'll see the title in the browser's title bar and your content in the browser window.

Understanding HTML Tags

In the example above, you used HTML tags to structure your content. Here's a brief explanation of the tags used:

- `<h1>`: This tag defines a top-level heading, usually used for the main title of your page.

- `<p>`: The paragraph tag is used for text content.

HTML Attributes

HTML tags can have attributes that provide additional information or properties. For example, the `<img>` tag uses the `src` attribute to specify the image source, and the `<a>` tag uses the `href` attribute to specify the hyperlink destination.

Conclusion

Congratulations! You've successfully created and viewed your first HTML page. You've learned the basic structure of an HTML document, how to add content, and how to view your web page in a browser.

In the next section, "1.5 Understanding the DOM (Document Object Model)," you'll delve into the concept of the Document Object Model and how JavaScript interacts with HTML elements to create dynamic web pages. Get ready to explore the core of web development!

1.5 Understanding the DOM (Document Object Model)

In this section, we will delve into the concept of the Document Object Model (DOM). The DOM is a critical aspect of web development as it represents the structure of web documents and enables you to interact with and manipulate web page elements using JavaScript.

What Is the DOM?

The Document Object Model (DOM) is a programming interface for web documents. It represents the structure and content of an HTML or XML document as a tree-like structure, where each element in the document is represented as a node in the tree. The DOM allows you to access and manipulate the content and structure of a web page dynamically.

Understanding DOM Nodes

In the DOM, everything is a node. Nodes can be of various types, but the most common ones you'll encounter are:

1. Element Nodes: These represent HTML elements, such as `<div>`, `<p>`, or `<a>`. Element nodes have properties and methods that allow you to modify their attributes and content.

2. Text Nodes: Text nodes contain the text within an HTML element. For example, the text inside a `<p>` element is contained within a text node.

3. Attribute Nodes: These represent attributes of HTML elements. For instance, the `src` attribute of an `<img>` element is an attribute node.

4. Document Nodes: The top-level node representing the entire document.

Accessing DOM Elements

To interact with and manipulate the DOM, JavaScript is commonly used. Here's how you can access DOM elements in JavaScript:

1. getElementById: You can select an element by its unique `id` attribute.

```javascript
const element = document.getElementById("myElementId");
```

2. getElementsByTagName: This method allows you to select elements by their tag name.

```javascript
const paragraphs = document.getElementsByTagName("p");
```

3. getElementsByClassName: You can select elements by their class name.

```javascript
const elementsWithClass = document.getElementsByClassName("myClass");
```

4. querySelector: This method allows you to use CSS-style selectors to select elements.

```javascript
const element = document.querySelector("#myElementId");
```

5. querySelectorAll: Similar to `querySelector`, but it selects all matching elements.

```javascript
const elements = document.querySelectorAll(".myClass");
```

Manipulating the DOM

Once you've selected a DOM element, you can manipulate it in various ways:

- **Changing Element Content:** You can change the content of an element, such as changing the text inside a `<p>` element.

- **Modifying Attributes:** You can change or add attributes to elements. For example, you can change the `src` attribute of an `<img>` element to change the displayed image.

- **Adding or Removing Elements:** You can create new elements and add them to the DOM or remove existing elements.

- Handling Events: You can attach event listeners to elements to respond to user interactions, like clicks or keypresses.

Practical Example

Let's consider a practical example. Suppose you have an HTML page with a button, and you want to change the text of a paragraph when the button is clicked. Here's how you can do it:

```html
<!DOCTYPE html>
<html>
 <body>
  <p id="myParagraph">This is a paragraph.</p>
  <button id="myButton">Change Text</button>

  <script>
   const paragraph = document.getElementById("myParagraph");
   const button = document.getElementById("myButton");

   button.addEventListener("click", function () {
    paragraph.textContent = "Text changed!";
   });
  </script>
 </body>
</html>
```

```

```

In this example, JavaScript code selects the paragraph and button elements using `getElementById`, adds an event listener to the button, and changes the text content of the paragraph when the button is clicked.

Understanding the DOM is crucial for creating dynamic and interactive web pages. It forms the foundation for building web applications that respond to user input and provide rich user experiences.

In the next section, "1.6 Basic HTML Elements," we will explore some common HTML elements and their uses in web development.

1.6 Basic HTML Elements

In this section, we will explore some of the fundamental HTML elements that are commonly used in web development. HTML (Hypertext Markup Language) provides a variety of elements to structure and display content on web pages.

1. Headings (`<h1>`, `<h2>`, `<h3>`, `<h4>`, `<h5>`, `<h6>`)

Headings are used to define the structure and hierarchy of content on a web page. They range from `<h1>` (the highest level, typically used for the main title) to `<h6>` (the lowest level, used for subsections).

Example:

```html
<h1>Main Heading</h1>
<h2>Subheading 1</h2>
<h3>Sub-subheading</h3>
<h2>Subheading 2</h2>
```

2. Paragraphs (`<p>`)

Paragraphs are used to represent text content. They create clear breaks between blocks of text.

Example:

```html
<p>This is a paragraph of text. It can contain multiple sentences and line breaks.</p>
```

3. Lists (`<ul>`, `<ol>`, `<li>`)

HTML supports both unordered lists (`<ul>`) and ordered lists (`<ol>`). List items are represented using `<li>` elements.

Unordered List (Bulleted):

```html
<ul>
  <li>Item 1</li>
  <li>Item 2</li>
  <li>Item 3</li>
</ul>
```

Ordered List (Numbered):

```html
<ol>
  <li>First Item</li>
```

```
  <li>Second Item</li>
  <li>Third Item</li>
</ol>
```

4. Links (`<a>`)

Anchor tags (`<a>`) are used to create hyperlinks to other web pages or resources.

Example:

```html
<a href="https://www.example.com">Visit Example.com</a>
```

5. Images (`<img>`)

The image element (`<img>`) is used to display images on a web page. It requires the `src` attribute, which specifies the image file's source.

Example:

```html
<img src="image.jpg" alt="Description of the image">
```

6. Divisions (`<div>`)

The division element (`<div>`) is a container used for grouping other elements. It is commonly used for layout and styling purposes.

Example:

```html
<div class="container">
  <p>This content is inside a div.</p>
</div>
```

7. Forms (`<form>`, `<input>`, `<button>`)

HTML forms (`<form>`) allow users to input data and submit it to a server. They typically contain form elements like text inputs (`<input>`), checkboxes, radio buttons, and buttons (`<button>`).

Example:

```html
<form>
  <label for="name">Name:</label>
  <input type="text" id="name" name="name">
```

```
  <br>
  <label for="email">Email:</label>
  <input type="email" id="email" name="email">
  <br>
  <button type="submit">Submit</button>
</form>
```

These are just a few of the basic HTML elements you'll use in web development. HTML provides a wide range of elements for various purposes, and as you progress in your web development journey, you'll learn how to use them effectively to create rich and interactive web pages.

In the next chapters, we'll explore more advanced HTML concepts, CSS for styling, and JavaScript for interactivity, enabling you to create dynamic and engaging web applications.

CHAPTER II
Styling Your Web Pages with CSS

2.1 Introduction to Cascading Style Sheets (CSS)

In this section, we will introduce you to the world of Cascading Style Sheets (CSS). CSS is a powerful language that allows you to control the presentation and layout of your web pages. It's an essential skill for any web developer.

What Is CSS?

Cascading Style Sheets (CSS) is a stylesheet language used to describe the look and formatting of a document written in HTML. CSS separates the content of a web page (HTML) from its presentation, enabling you to control the visual aspects of your web pages.

Why Use CSS?

CSS offers several advantages for web development:

1. Separation of Concerns: CSS separates the structure (HTML) from the style (CSS) and behavior (JavaScript) of a web page. This separation makes your code more organized and maintainable.

2. Consistency: CSS allows you to create consistent styles across multiple pages of a website. You can define styles in one place and apply them universally.

3. Flexibility: With CSS, you can control the layout, colors, typography, and other visual aspects of your web pages. This flexibility allows for creative and customized designs.

CSS Syntax

CSS uses a simple syntax that consists of selectors and declarations. Here's a basic example:

```css
/* This is a CSS comment */
selector {
  property: value;
}
```

- **Selector:** A selector is used to target HTML elements to which you want to apply styles. Selectors can be element names (e.g., `h1`, `p`), class names (e.g., `.my-class`), IDs (e.g., `#my-id`), or more complex patterns.

- **Property:** A property defines the aspect of an element you want to style, such as `color`, `font-size`, or `background-color`.

- **Value:** The value specifies the style's value for the selected property (e.g., `red`, `16px`, `#F0F0F0`).

Adding CSS to HTML

You can include CSS in your HTML documents in several ways:

1. Inline Styles: You can add styles directly to HTML elements using the `style` attribute.

```html
<p style="color: blue;">This is a blue paragraph.</p>
```

2. Internal Stylesheet: You can define CSS styles within the HTML document using the `<style>` element in the document's `<head>` section.

```html
<head>
 <style>
  p {
   color: green;
  }
 </style>
</head>
<body>
 <p>This is a green paragraph.</p>
</body>
```

3. External Stylesheet: You can create a separate `.css` file and link it to your HTML document using the `<link>` element.

```html
<head>
  <link rel="stylesheet" type="text/css" href="styles.css">
</head>
```

In the `styles.css` file:

```css
p {
  font-size: 18px;
}
```

CSS Comments

Comments in CSS are important for adding notes and explanations to your code. CSS comments start with `/*` and end with `*/`.

```css
/* This is a CSS comment */
```

```
p {
  color: orange;
}
```
```

## Conclusion

This introduction has given you a glimpse into the world of CSS. You've learned what CSS is, why it's important, and the basic syntax for writing CSS rules. In the upcoming sections, we'll dive deeper into CSS, covering selectors, properties, values, and various techniques to style your web pages effectively. Get ready to make your web pages visually appealing and engaging!
```

2.2 Selectors and Styles

In this section, we'll explore CSS selectors and styles in detail. Selectors allow you to target specific HTML elements, and styles define how those elements should appear on your web page.

CSS Selectors

CSS selectors are patterns used to select and style HTML elements. They determine which elements the styles should be applied to. Here are some common types of CSS selectors:

1. Element Selector: Targets all elements of a specific type.

```css
p {
  color: blue;
}
```

2. Class Selector: Targets elements with a specific class attribute.

```css
.highlight {
  background-color: yellow;
}
```

3. ID Selector: Targets a single element with a specific ID attribute.

```css
#header {
  font-size: 24px;
}
```

4. Descendant Selector: Targets elements that are descendants of a specific element.

```css
article p {
  font-style: italic;
}
```

5. Child Selector: Targets elements that are direct children of a specific element.

```css
ul > li {
  list-style-type: square;
}
```

6. Attribute Selector: Targets elements with a specific attribute.

```css
input[type="text"] {
  border: 1px solid #ccc;
}
```

7. Pseudo-class Selector: Targets elements based on their state or position.

```css
a:hover {
  text-decoration: underline;
}
```

8. Pseudo-element Selector: Targets a specific part of an element.

```css
p::first-line {
  font-weight: bold;
}
```

CSS Styles

Once you've selected elements using CSS selectors, you can apply styles to them using CSS properties and values. Here are some common CSS properties and values:

- **Color Properties:** `color`, `background-color`, `border-color`, etc.

- **Text Properties:** `font-family`, `font-size`, `text-align`, etc.

- **Layout Properties:** `width`, `height`, `margin`, `padding`, `display`, etc.

- **Positioning Properties:** `position`, `top`, `left`, `z-index`, etc.

- **Transform and Animation Properties:** `transform`, `animation`, `transition`, etc.

Combining Selectors

You can combine multiple selectors to apply styles to specific elements. For example:

```css
h1, h2, h3 {
  font-family: Arial, sans-serif;
}
```

This rule sets the font family for all `h1`, `h2`, and `h3` elements.

Specificity

CSS selectors have specificity, which determines which styles take precedence when multiple styles conflict. Understanding specificity is essential for controlling style application.

Example:

Let's say you want to style all paragraphs within a div with the class "content":

```css
div.content p {
  font-size: 16px;
  color: #333;
}
```

In this example, we use the descendant selector to select all `<p>` elements within a `<div>` with the class "content." We then set the font size and color for those paragraphs.

Conclusion

In this section, you've learned about CSS selectors and styles. CSS selectors help you target specific HTML elements, and CSS properties and values allow you to define how those elements should be styled. Understanding how to select and style elements is fundamental to creating visually appealing web pages.

In the next sections, we'll dive deeper into CSS properties and values, explore techniques for creating layouts, and understand the CSS box model, which is crucial for web page design.

2.3 CSS Properties and Values

In this section, we'll dive into CSS properties and values, providing a comprehensive overview of the essential aspects of styling your web pages with CSS.

Understanding CSS Properties and Values

CSS properties define the characteristics of HTML elements, while values determine the specific settings for those properties. Here, we'll explore some commonly used CSS properties and their associated values:

1. Color Properties:

- `color`: Sets the text color.

- `background-color`: Defines the background color.

Example:
```css
p {
  color: #333;
  background-color: #f0f0f0;
}
```

2. Typography Properties:

- `font-family`: Specifies the font.

- `font-size`: Sets the font size.

- `font-weight`: Defines the font weight (e.g., bold, normal).

Example:
```css
h1 {
  font-family: "Arial", sans-serif;
  font-size: 24px;
  font-weight: bold;
}
```

3. Layout Properties:

- `width`: Defines the width of an element.

- `height`: Specifies the height of an element.

- `margin`: Sets the margin around an element.

- `padding`: Defines the padding within an element.

Example:
```css
.container {
  width: 80%;
  margin: 0 auto;
```

```
  padding: 10px;

}
```

4. Border and Outline Properties:

- `border`: Defines the border properties.

- `outline`: Sets an outline around an element (often used for focus styles).

Example:
```css
button {

  border: 2px solid #007bff;

  outline: none;

}
```

5. Positioning and Layout Properties:

- `position`: Specifies the positioning method (e.g., relative, absolute).

- `top`, `bottom`, `left`, `right`: Defines the position of an element when using `position: absolute` or `position: fixed`.

- `display`: Specifies how an element should be displayed (e.g., `block`, `inline`, `flex`).

Example:

```css
.header {
  position: fixed;
  top: 0;
  left: 0;
  width: 100%;
}
```

Shorthand Properties

CSS also provides shorthand properties that allow you to set multiple related properties with a single declaration. For example, `margin` and `padding` properties have shorthand forms:

- `margin`: Sets margins for all four sides (top, right, bottom, left) in one declaration.
- `padding`: Sets padding for all four sides in one declaration.

Example:
```css
.box {
  margin: 10px 20px 10px 30px; /* top right bottom left */
  padding: 5px 10px; /* top/bottom left/right */
}
```

Conclusion

In this section, we've explored fundamental CSS properties and values. Understanding how to use these properties is crucial for controlling the appearance and layout of your web pages. As you progress in your web development journey, you'll discover many more CSS properties and values that allow you to create intricate and visually appealing designs.

In the upcoming sections, we'll cover how to add these styles to HTML elements, create complex layouts with CSS, and delve into the CSS box model, which is essential for understanding how elements are sized and spaced on a web page.

2.4 Adding Styles to HTML Elements

In this section, we'll explore various methods for adding styles to HTML elements using CSS. Styling is a crucial part of web development, and understanding how to apply styles to your HTML elements is essential.

Inline Styles

The most basic way to add styles to an HTML element is by using inline styles. Inline styles are defined directly within the HTML element's tag using the `style` attribute.

Example:

```html
<p style="color: blue; font-size: 16px;">This is a blue paragraph.</p>
```

Inline styles are useful for quick styling but can become hard to manage when you have many elements with similar styles.

Internal Stylesheets

You can also include CSS styles directly within your HTML document using the `<style>` element within the document's `<head>` section. This method is known as using an internal stylesheet.

Example:

```html
```

```
<!DOCTYPE html>
<html>
<head>
  <style>
  p {
    color: green;
    font-size: 18px;
  }
  </style>
</head>
<body>
  <p>This is a green paragraph.</p>
</body>
</html>
```

Internal stylesheets allow you to define styles that apply to multiple elements on the same page. However, they are still limited to a single HTML document.

External Stylesheets

To keep your CSS separate from your HTML and make styles reusable across multiple pages, you can use external stylesheets. An external stylesheet is a separate `.css` file linked to your HTML document using the `<link>` element.

Example:

In your HTML file (`index.html`):

```html
<!DOCTYPE html>
<html>
<head>
  <link rel="stylesheet" type="text/css" href="styles.css">
</head>
<body>
  <p class="highlight">This is a styled paragraph.</p>
</body>
</html>
```

In your CSS file (`styles.css`):

```css
/* styles.css */
.highlight {
  background-color: yellow;
  font-weight: bold;
}
```

Using external stylesheets is the preferred method for adding styles to your web pages because it promotes maintainability and reusability. You can link the same stylesheet to multiple HTML documents, ensuring a consistent look and feel across your entire website.

Conclusion

In this section, we've explored different methods for adding styles to HTML elements using CSS. Whether you choose inline styles, internal stylesheets, or external stylesheets depends on your project's needs and complexity. External stylesheets are recommended for larger projects, as they provide better organization and consistency across your website.

In the next sections, we'll delve into creating layouts with CSS and understanding the CSS box model, which are essential aspects of web page design and styling.

2.5 Creating Layouts with CSS

In this section, we'll delve into the art of creating layouts with CSS. Web page layouts define the structure and positioning of elements on a web page, and CSS plays a pivotal role in achieving these layouts.

Understanding Layout Principles

Before we dive into specific CSS techniques for layout, it's essential to understand some fundamental layout principles:

1. Box Model: In CSS, every element is considered a rectangular box. The box model includes properties like `width`, `height`, `margin`, `padding`, and `border`. Understanding how these properties affect the layout is crucial.

2. Display Property: The `display` property defines how an element should be displayed. Common values include `block`, `inline`, `inline-block`, and `flex`. Each value has unique layout characteristics.

3. Positioning: CSS offers various positioning options, such as `relative`, `absolute`, and `fixed`. These properties enable you to control the placement of elements within the layout.

4. Floats: The `float` property allows elements to float to the left or right within their parent container. It's often used for creating multi-column layouts.

Creating a Simple Two-Column Layout

Let's create a basic two-column layout as an example. In this layout, we'll have a header, a sidebar, and a content area. We'll use CSS to achieve this structure:

HTML:

````html
<!DOCTYPE html>
<html>
<head>
  <link rel="stylesheet" type="text/css" href="styles.css">
</head>
<body>
  <header>
   <h1>Website Header</h1>
  </header>
  <aside class="sidebar">
   <h2>Sidebar</h2>
   <ul>
    <li>Link 1</li>
    <li>Link 2</li>
    <li>Link 3</li>
   </ul>
  </aside>
  <main class="content">
   <h2>Main Content</h2>
   <p>This is the main content area.</p>
````

```
    </main>
  </body>
</html>
```

CSS (`styles.css`):
```css
/* Reset some default styles and apply a basic layout */
body {
  margin: 0;
  padding: 0;
  font-family: Arial, sans-serif;
}

/* Header styles */
header {
  background-color: #333;
  color: #fff;
  text-align: center;
  padding: 10px 0;
}

/* Sidebar styles */
.sidebar {
  float: left;
```

```
  width: 20%;

  background-color: #f0f0f0;

  padding: 20px;

}


/* Main content styles */

.content {

  margin-left: 22%; /* Adjust for the width of the sidebar */

  padding: 20px;

}
```
```

This example demonstrates a simple two-column layout with a header, sidebar, and content area. CSS properties like `float`, `width`, and `margin` are used to control the layout.


**Conclusion**


Creating layouts with CSS is a fundamental skill for web developers. In this section, we've touched on some key layout principles and provided an example of a basic two-column layout. As you explore more complex web page designs, you'll encounter additional CSS techniques and frameworks for creating responsive and intricate layouts.


In the next section, we'll delve deeper into the CSS box model, which is essential for understanding how elements are sized and spaced within your web page layout.
```

2.6 CSS Box Model

In this section, we'll dive deep into the CSS Box Model, a fundamental concept that governs how elements are sized and spaced on a web page. Understanding the Box Model is crucial for precise control over your web page layout.

What is the CSS Box Model?

The CSS Box Model is a conceptual representation of how every HTML element is treated as a rectangular box. This box consists of four crucial components:

1. **Content:** The actual content of the element, such as text or images.

2. **Padding:** The space between the content and the element's border. Padding can be specified using properties like `padding-top`, `padding-right`, `padding-bottom`, and `padding-left`.

3. **Border:** A line that surrounds the element's padding. Borders can be customized using properties like `border-width`, `border-style`, and `border-color`.

4. **Margin:** The space between the element's border and adjacent elements. Margins can be specified using properties like `margin-top`, `margin-right`, `margin-bottom`, and `margin-left`.

Calculating the Total Element Size

To calculate the total size of an element, you need to consider the following:

```
```

Total Width = Width + (Left Padding + Right Padding) + (Left Border + Right Border) + (Left Margin + Right Margin)

Total Height = Height + (Top Padding + Bottom Padding) + (Top Border + Bottom Border) + (Top Margin + Bottom Margin)

```

**Example:**

Let's say you have a `div` element with the following CSS:

```css
div {
  width: 200px;
  height: 100px;
  padding: 10px;
  border: 2px solid #333;
  margin: 20px;
}
```

In this case:

- `Width` and `Height` are 200px and 100px, respectively.

- `Padding` adds 10px to both the width and height.

- `Border` adds 4px (2px on each side) to both the width and height.
```

- `Margin` adds 40px (20px on each side) to both the width and height.

So, the total width of the `div` is `200px + 10px + 4px + 20px = 234px`, and the total height is `100px + 10px + 4px + 20px = 134px`.

Box Model in Practice

Understanding the CSS Box Model is essential when designing web page layouts. You use padding, border, and margin properties to create spacing and structure, ensuring elements are positioned as intended.

Conclusion

In this section, we've explored the CSS Box Model, a fundamental concept in web development. Understanding how elements are sized and spaced within this model is crucial for achieving precise control over your web page layout.

In the upcoming chapters, we'll continue to explore advanced CSS techniques, responsive design, and other essential topics in web development.

CHAPTER III
JavaScript Essentials

3.1 Introduction to JavaScript

JavaScript is a versatile and widely used programming language in web development. In this section, we'll provide a comprehensive introduction to JavaScript, covering its core concepts and how to use it in web development.

What Is JavaScript?

JavaScript, often abbreviated as JS, is a high-level, interpreted programming language primarily used for adding interactivity to web pages. Unlike HTML and CSS, which focus on structure and presentation, respectively, JavaScript is all about behavior.

Key Concepts in JavaScript

Let's dive into some key concepts in JavaScript:

1. Variables and Data Types: JavaScript allows you to declare variables to store data. It supports various data types, including numbers, strings, booleans, arrays, and objects.

2. Operators and Expressions: You can perform operations on data using operators such as `+` (addition), `-` (subtraction), `*` (multiplication), `/` (division), and `%` (modulo).

3. Control Structures: JavaScript provides conditional statements like `if`, `else`, and `switch` for making decisions in your code. Loops like `for`, `while`, and `do...while` allow you to repeat actions.

4. Functions: Functions are blocks of reusable code that can be defined and called to perform specific tasks. JavaScript also supports anonymous functions and arrow functions.

5. Scope: Understanding scope is crucial. Variables can have local or global scope, affecting their accessibility within your code.

Using JavaScript in Web Development

JavaScript can be embedded directly into HTML documents using `<script>` tags or included from external files. It allows you to:

- Modify HTML: You can change the content and structure of HTML elements dynamically, responding to user interactions or other events.

- Interact with the Browser: JavaScript provides methods to manipulate browser behavior, such as opening new windows, handling cookies, and detecting user input.

- Asynchronous Operations: You can perform asynchronous operations like making network requests (AJAX) or handling timers using JavaScript.

Example: Basic JavaScript Code

Here's a simple example of JavaScript code that displays a message when a button is clicked:

```html
<!DOCTYPE html>
<html>
<head>
  <title>JavaScript Example</title>
</head>
<body>
  <button id="myButton">Click me</button>
  <script>
    // Get the button element by its id
    var button = document.getElementById("myButton");

    // Add a click event listener
    button.addEventListener("click", function() {
      alert("Hello, JavaScript!");
    });
  </script>
</body>
</html>
```

In this example, JavaScript is used to add an event listener to the button element. When clicked, it triggers an alert with the message "Hello, JavaScript!"

Conclusion

JavaScript is a powerful language that brings interactivity and dynamic behavior to web pages. In this section, we've introduced the fundamental concepts of JavaScript. In the following chapters, we'll delve deeper into variables, control structures, functions, and other essential aspects of JavaScript programming.

3.2 Variables and Data Types

In JavaScript, variables are fundamental for storing and managing data. Understanding variables and data types is crucial for writing effective code. In this section, we'll explore variables, data types, and how to use them in JavaScript.

What Are Variables?

Variables are containers for storing data values. Think of them as named storage locations in your code. You can assign values to variables, and those values can change over time. Variables provide flexibility and dynamism to your JavaScript programs.

Declaring Variables

In JavaScript, you can declare variables using the `var`, `let`, or `const` keyword. Here's a brief overview of each:

- `var`: Historically used to declare variables in JavaScript, but it has some scope-related quirks. It's less commonly used in modern JavaScript.

- `let`: Introduced in ECMAScript 6 (ES6), `let` allows you to declare variables with block scope. It's suitable for most use cases.

- `const`: Also introduced in ES6, `const` is used to declare variables whose values should not change once assigned. It also has block scope.

Data Types

JavaScript supports several data types:

1. Primitive Data Types: These are the basic building blocks of data.

  - `Number`: Represents numeric values, including integers and floating-point numbers.

  - `String`: Represents text and is enclosed in single or double quotes.

  - `Boolean`: Represents true or false values.

  - `Null`: Represents the intentional absence of any object value.

  - `Undefined`: Represents an uninitialized variable.

2. Complex Data Types: These are more advanced data structures.

  - `Object`: Represents a collection of key-value pairs, similar to dictionaries in other languages.

  - `Array`: Represents an ordered list of values, which can be of different data types.

  - `Function`: Represents reusable blocks of code.

Example: Declaring Variables and Data Types

Here's an example of declaring variables with different data types:

```javascript
let age = 25; // Number
let name = "John"; // String
let isStudent = true; // Boolean
let grades = [90, 85, 88]; // Array
```

```
let person = { firstName: "John", lastName: "Doe" }; // Object

let greet = function() {

  console.log("Hello, World!");

}; // Function

```
```

In this example, we've declared variables with various data types, including numbers, strings, booleans, an array, an object, and a function.

Conclusion

Understanding variables and data types is essential for working with JavaScript. In this section, we've explored the basics of declaring variables and the various data types available in JavaScript. In the following chapters, we'll delve deeper into JavaScript's capabilities, including operators, control structures, functions, and more.
```

3.3 Operators and Expressions

Operators and expressions are fundamental concepts in JavaScript, allowing you to perform various operations and calculations. In this section, we'll explore different types of operators and how to use them in expressions.

What Are Operators?

Operators are symbols or keywords in JavaScript that perform operations on values or variables. They are the building blocks for creating expressions, which are combinations of values, variables, and operators that produce a result.

Types of Operators

JavaScript supports several types of operators:

1. Arithmetic Operators: These operators perform mathematical calculations.

- `+` (Addition): Adds two numbers.
- `-` (Subtraction): Subtracts the right operand from the left operand.
- `*` (Multiplication): Multiplies two numbers.
- `/` (Division): Divides the left operand by the right operand.
- `%` (Modulo): Returns the remainder of a division operation.

2. Comparison Operators: These operators compare two values and return a Boolean result.

- `==` (Equal to): Checks if two values are equal.

- `!=` (Not equal to): Checks if two values are not equal.

- `>` (Greater than): Checks if the left operand is greater than the right operand.

- `<` (Less than): Checks if the left operand is less than the right operand.

- `>=` (Greater than or equal to): Checks if the left operand is greater than or equal to the right operand.

- `<=` (Less than or equal to): Checks if the left operand is less than or equal to the right operand.

3. Logical Operators: These operators perform logical operations and return a Boolean result.

- `&&` (Logical AND): Returns true if both operands are true.

- `||` (Logical OR): Returns true if at least one operand is true.

- `!` (Logical NOT): Returns the opposite Boolean value of the operand.

4. Assignment Operators: These operators assign values to variables.

- `=` (Assignment): Assigns the value on the right to the variable on the left.

- `+=` (Addition assignment): Adds the right operand to the variable on the left and assigns the result.

- `-=` (Subtraction assignment): Subtracts the right operand from the variable on the left and assigns the result.

- `*=` (Multiplication assignment): Multiplies the variable on the left by the right operand and assigns the result.

5. Other Operators: JavaScript also includes the `typeof` operator (used to determine the data type of a value) and the ternary operator (`? :`) for conditional expressions.

Example: Using Operators in Expressions

Here are some examples of using operators in expressions:

```javascript
let x = 5;
let y = 3;

let sum = x + y; // sum is 8
let isGreater = x > y; // isGreater is true
let result = (x * 2) + (y / 2); // result is 11.5
```

In these examples, we've used arithmetic, comparison, and assignment operators to perform various operations.

Conclusion

Operators and expressions are essential for performing calculations and making decisions in JavaScript. In this section, we've covered different types of operators and how to use them in expressions. In the following chapters, we'll explore control structures, functions, and other key JavaScript concepts.

3.4 Control Structures: Conditional Statements and Loops

Control structures are essential in programming as they allow you to make decisions and repeat actions based on conditions. In JavaScript, you can use conditional statements and loops to control the flow of your code.

Conditional Statements

Conditional statements allow you to execute different code blocks based on specified conditions. JavaScript provides several types of conditional statements:

1. if Statement: The `if` statement is used to execute a block of code if a specified condition is true.

```javascript
if (condition) {
  // Code to execute if the condition is true
} else {
  // Code to execute if the condition is false
}
```

2. else Statement: You can use the `else` statement to specify a block of code to execute if the condition in the `if` statement is false.

3. else if Statement: The `else if` statement allows you to specify multiple conditions to check.

```javascript
if (condition1) {
  // Code to execute if condition1 is true
} else if (condition2) {
  // Code to execute if condition2 is true
} else {
  // Code to execute if neither condition1 nor condition2 is true
}
```

Loops

Loops are used to execute a block of code repeatedly. JavaScript supports various types of loops:

1. for Loop: The `for` loop is used to execute a block of code a specified number of times.

```javascript
for (initialization; condition; iteration) {
  // Code to execute in each iteration
}
```

2. while Loop: The `while` loop continues executing a block of code as long as a specified condition is true.

```javascript
while (condition) {

  // Code to execute as long as the condition is true

}
```

3. do...while Loop: The `do...while` loop is similar to the `while` loop, but it guarantees that the block of code is executed at least once, even if the condition is initially false.

```javascript
do {

  // Code to execute at least once

} while (condition);
```

Example: Using Conditional Statements and Loops

Here's an example that demonstrates the use of conditional statements and loops:

```javascript
let count = 5;

if (count > 0) {

  console.log("Count is positive.");
```

```javascript
} else if (count < 0) {
  console.log("Count is negative.");
} else {
  console.log("Count is zero.");
}


for (let i = 0; i < 5; i++) {
  console.log("Iteration " + i);
}


let i = 0;
while (i < 3) {
  console.log("While loop iteration " + i);
  i++;
}
```
```

In this example, we use conditional statements (`if`, `else if`, and `else`) and loops (`for` and `while`) to control the flow of the program based on conditions.


**Conclusion**


Control structures, including conditional statements and loops, are fundamental for writing dynamic JavaScript code. In this section, we've explored how to use these structures to make decisions and repeat actions in your programs. In the next chapter, we'll dive into functions and scope, another critical aspect of JavaScript programming.
```

3.5 Functions and Scope

Functions are the building blocks of JavaScript. They allow you to group code into reusable blocks, making your code more organized and efficient. In this section, we'll explore JavaScript functions and how they work, including their scope and common use cases.

Functions in JavaScript

A function is a block of code that can be defined and called later in your program. Functions are defined using the `function` keyword, followed by a name and a set of parentheses. They can also accept parameters, which act as placeholders for values passed to the function.

Here's the basic syntax of a JavaScript function:

```javascript
function functionName(parameter1, parameter2, ...) {
  // Function code
  return result; // Optional return statement
}
```

- `functionName`: The name of the function.

- `parameter1`, `parameter2`, ...: Parameters that the function can accept.

- `return result`: An optional `return` statement to return a value from the function.

Function Scope

JavaScript has two types of scope: global and local. When you declare a variable inside a function using the `var`, `let`, or `const` keyword, that variable is considered to have local scope and is accessible only within that function. Variables declared outside of any function have global scope and can be accessed from anywhere in your code.

Example: Creating and Using Functions

Let's look at an example of how to create and use functions in JavaScript:

```javascript
// Function declaration
function greet(name) {
  return "Hello, " + name + "!";
}

// Function call
let message = greet("John");
console.log(message); // Output: "Hello, John!"
```

In this example, we define a function `greet` that takes a `name` parameter and returns a greeting message. We then call the function with the argument `"John"` and store the result in the `message` variable.

Function Expression

Functions can also be defined as expressions and assigned to variables. These are called function expressions. They are useful for creating anonymous functions and passing them as arguments to other functions.

```javascript
const add = function (a, b) {
  return a + b;
};

let result = add(2, 3); // result is 5
```

Conclusion

Functions are a fundamental concept in JavaScript programming. They allow you to encapsulate logic into reusable blocks of code. Understanding function scope, parameters, and return values is crucial for writing effective JavaScript programs. In the next section, we'll delve into handling events and user interactions, enabling you to create interactive web applications.

3.6 Handling Events and User Interactions

JavaScript is not limited to manipulating data and creating logic; it's also essential for making your web pages interactive. This section will introduce you to handling events and user interactions in JavaScript, allowing you to create dynamic and responsive web applications.

Events in JavaScript

Events are actions or occurrences that happen in the browser, such as a user clicking a button, moving the mouse, or typing on the keyboard. JavaScript allows you to respond to these events by executing code in response to them. This interaction is what makes web pages feel dynamic.

Here's a basic example of handling a click event:

```javascript
// Get a reference to an HTML element
const button = document.querySelector('button');

// Add a click event listener to the button
button.addEventListener('click', function() {
  alert('Button clicked!');
});
```

In this example, we select an HTML button element using `querySelector` and attach a click event listener to it. When the button is clicked, the provided function is executed, displaying an alert.

Common DOM Events

JavaScript provides a wide range of events to work with, such as:

- Click events

- Mouseover and mouseout events

- Keyboard events

- Form events (submit, input, change)

- Window events (load, resize, scroll)

Event Handling Functions

Event handling functions take an event object as a parameter, which contains information about the event, such as the target element, event type, and any data related to the event. You can use this information to customize your event handlers.

Example: Handling a Form Submit Event

```javascript
const form = document.querySelector('form');

form.addEventListener('submit', function(event) {
  event.preventDefault(); // Prevent the default form submission
  const inputValue = event.target.querySelector('input').value;
```

```
  alert('You submitted: ' + inputValue);

});

```
```

In this example, we prevent the default form submission behavior, access the input value, and display it in an alert when the form is submitted.

Interactive Web Applications

By mastering event handling, you can create interactive web applications that respond to user actions in real-time. This capability is the foundation of many modern web applications, from simple form validation to complex interactive games.

Understanding how to handle events and user interactions is crucial as you continue your journey into web development. It's a skill that opens up a world of possibilities for creating engaging and dynamic web experiences.
```

CHAPTER IV
Building Interactive Web Pages

4.1 DOM Manipulation with JavaScript

In web development, the Document Object Model (DOM) is a crucial concept. The DOM represents the structure of a web page and allows you to interact with and manipulate its elements using JavaScript. In this section, we'll dive into the fundamentals of DOM manipulation and how to use JavaScript to change and interact with web page elements.

What is the DOM?

The DOM is a hierarchical tree-like structure that represents the elements of an HTML document. Each element, such as headings, paragraphs, images, and buttons, is a part of this tree. JavaScript provides a way to access and modify this tree, enabling dynamic web page interactions.

Accessing DOM Elements

You can access DOM elements using JavaScript by selecting them based on their HTML tags, IDs, classes, or other attributes. Here's how you can access an element with an ID:

```javascript
const element = document.getElementById('elementId');
```

Modifying DOM Elements

Once you've selected a DOM element, you can manipulate it in various ways. For example, you can change its text content, modify its attributes, or even add or remove elements. Here's an example that changes the text content of a paragraph:

```javascript
const paragraph = document.getElementById('myParagraph');
paragraph.textContent = 'New text content';
```

Creating and Adding DOM Elements

JavaScript also allows you to create new DOM elements and add them to the page. For instance, you can create a new `div` element and append it to the `body` of your HTML document:

```javascript
const newDiv = document.createElement('div');
newDiv.textContent = 'This is a new div';
document.body.appendChild(newDiv);
```

Event Handling with DOM

Events play a vital role in web interactivity. You can use event listeners to respond to various user interactions, such as clicks, key presses, or mouse movements. Here's an example of adding a click event listener to a button:

```javascript
const button = document.getElementById('myButton');

button.addEventListener('click', function() {

  alert('Button clicked!');

});
```

Benefits of DOM Manipulation

- **Dynamic Interactions:** DOM manipulation allows you to create dynamic and responsive web applications.

- **User Engagement:** You can enhance user engagement by creating interactive features like forms, buttons, and animations.

- **Real-time Updates:** Websites can update content in real-time without requiring a full page reload.

- **Improved User Experience:** By providing a seamless and interactive experience, users are more likely to stay engaged with your website.

Understanding DOM manipulation is a key skill for web developers, as it forms the foundation for building interactive and dynamic web pages. In the next sections, we'll explore event handling and creating dynamic content to further enhance your web development capabilities.

4.2 Event Handling and Event Listeners

Web applications become interactive by responding to user actions, and that's where event handling comes into play. Events are user interactions like clicks, keypresses, or mouse movements. In this section, we'll delve into event handling and event listeners, essential for creating engaging web pages.

Understanding Events

Events are actions or occurrences that happen in the browser, like a user clicking a button or moving the mouse. To make your web page responsive, you need to set up event listeners to detect these actions and trigger specific functions when they occur.

Adding Event Listeners

To respond to an event, you attach an event listener to a DOM element. Event listeners "listen" for specific events on an element and execute a function (an event handler) when that event occurs. Here's how to add a click event listener to a button:

```javascript
const button = document.getElementById('myButton');

button.addEventListener('click', function() {
  // Your code to handle the click event goes here
});
```

Commonly Used Events

There are various events you can listen for, depending on the user's actions and interactions. Some common events include:

- `click`: Triggered when an element is clicked.

- `keydown` and `keyup`: Fired when a key is pressed and released, respectively.

- `mouseover` and `mouseout`: Occur when the mouse enters and exits an element.

- `submit`: Fired when a form is submitted.

Event Object

When an event occurs, an event object is automatically created and passed to the event handler function. This object contains information about the event, such as the target element and event type. Here's an example of using the event object to get the clicked element:

```javascript
button.addEventListener('click', function(event) {
  const clickedElement = event.target;
  // Your code to handle the click event using the event object goes here
});
```

Event Propagation

Events can propagate through the DOM tree, either through capturing (from the outermost ancestor to the target element) or bubbling (from the target element back up to the ancestor). You can control this behavior using the `addEventListener` method's third parameter (`useCapture`).

Benefits of Event Handling

- **Interactivity:** Event handling enables your web page to respond to user actions, creating interactive user interfaces.

- **Real-time Updates:** You can provide real-time updates and feedback to users.

- **Enhanced User Experience:** Well-handled events improve the overall user experience by making your web page more engaging and user-friendly.

Understanding event handling and event listeners is pivotal for building interactive web applications. In the upcoming sections, we'll explore creating dynamic content, form validation, and working with images and media to further enhance your web development skills.

4.3 Creating Dynamic Content

One of the most compelling aspects of web development is the ability to create dynamic and interactive content that can change and adapt based on user actions and data. In this section, we will explore how to create dynamic content using JavaScript.

Understanding Dynamic Content

Dynamic content refers to web page elements that can change without requiring a full page reload. This dynamic behavior is typically achieved through JavaScript, which can manipulate the Document Object Model (DOM) of a web page.

Manipulating the DOM

The DOM represents the structure of a web page, and JavaScript allows you to manipulate it in real-time. Here are some common tasks related to creating dynamic content:

1. Creating Elements: You can use JavaScript to create new HTML elements dynamically. For example, you can create new paragraphs, divs, or list items.

```javascript
const newParagraph = document.createElement('p');
newParagraph.textContent = 'This is a new paragraph.';
```

2. Modifying Content: JavaScript can change the content of existing elements. You can update text, attributes, or even HTML structure.

```javascript
const heading = document.querySelector('h1');

heading.textContent = 'Updated Heading';
```

3. Adding and Removing Elements: You can add new elements to the DOM or remove existing ones. This is particularly useful for things like adding or removing items from a list.

```javascript
const list = document.getElementById('myList');

const newItem = document.createElement('li');

newItem.textContent = 'New List Item';

list.appendChild(newItem); // Add item

list.removeChild(existingItem); // Remove item
```

Event-Driven Dynamic Content

Dynamic content often responds to user interactions. You can combine event handling, as discussed in the previous section, with dynamic content to create interactive web applications. For example, you can update the content of a webpage when a user clicks a button.

```javascript
const button = document.getElementById('myButton');

button.addEventListener('click', function() {
```

```
const paragraph = document.createElement('p');

paragraph.textContent = 'New content added!';

document.body.appendChild(paragraph);

});
```
```

**Benefits of Dynamic Content**

- **Real-Time Updates:** Dynamic content provides real-time updates to users, making web applications more interactive.

- **Improved User Experience:** By updating content without page reloads, you enhance the user experience.

- **Data-Driven Interfaces:** Dynamic content is often driven by data from APIs or databases, allowing for dynamic data rendering.

Creating dynamic content is a fundamental skill in web development, enabling you to build responsive and interactive web applications. In the next sections, we'll explore form validation, user feedback, and working with images and media to further enrich your web development toolkit.
```

4.4 Form Validation and User Feedback

Forms are a crucial part of web applications, allowing users to input data and interact with websites. However, it's essential to ensure that the data submitted through forms is valid and meets your application's requirements. In this section, we will explore form validation and providing user feedback for a better user experience.

Understanding Form Validation

Form validation is the process of checking user input to ensure that it meets specified criteria before it's submitted to the server. This helps prevent incorrect or malicious data from being processed. Common use cases for form validation include:

- Checking that required fields are not empty.

- Validating email addresses, phone numbers, or other specific formats.

- Verifying that numeric inputs are within specified ranges.

- Confirming that passwords meet security requirements.

HTML5 Form Validation

HTML5 introduced built-in form validation features that browsers can enforce without JavaScript. You can use attributes like `required`, `type`, and `pattern` on form elements to specify validation rules. For example:

```html
<form>
  <label for="email">Email:</label>
```

```
  <input type="email" id="email" name="email" required>
  <input type="submit" value="Submit">
</form>
```

In this example, the `type="email"` attribute tells the browser to validate the input as an email address, and the `required` attribute makes the field mandatory.

JavaScript Form Validation

While HTML5 provides basic form validation, you may need more complex validation rules. JavaScript allows you to implement custom validation logic. Here's an example of JavaScript-based form validation:

```javascript
const form = document.getElementById('myForm');
const emailInput = document.getElementById('email');

form.addEventListener('submit', function(event) {
  if (!isValidEmail(emailInput.value)) {
    event.preventDefault(); // Prevent form submission
    alert('Please enter a valid email address.');
  }
});

function isValidEmail(email) {
```

```
  // Implement email validation logic

  // Return true if valid, false otherwise

}
```
```

In this code, we use JavaScript to add a custom event listener to the form's submit event. If the email input doesn't meet the validation criteria, we prevent the form from submitting and provide feedback to the user.

## User Feedback

User feedback is crucial to inform users about validation results. You can provide feedback in various ways, such as:

- Displaying error messages next to the problematic fields.

- Highlighting the fields with invalid data.

- Using tooltips or pop-up messages.

- Providing real-time validation as users type.

Remember that effective form validation not only prevents incorrect data but also helps users understand what went wrong and how to fix it.

By implementing form validation and user feedback, you can create web forms that are user-friendly, secure, and minimize errors in user-submitted data. In the next section, we'll explore working with images and media to enhance your web applications further.
```

4.5 Working with Images and Media

In this section, we'll explore how to work with images and media elements in web development. Images and media can greatly enhance the user experience on your website. We'll cover topics such as inserting images, embedding audio and video, optimizing media for the web, and responsive design.

Inserting Images

Images are often used to make web content more visually appealing. To insert images into your web pages, you can use the HTML `<img>` element. Here's an example:

```html
<img src="image.jpg" alt="A beautiful landscape">
```

- The `src` attribute specifies the path to the image file.

- The `alt` attribute provides alternative text for screen readers and browsers that cannot display the image.

You can also control the size of images using CSS or HTML attributes like `width` and `height`.

Optimizing Images

Optimizing images is essential for improving website performance. Large images can slow down page loading times. You can optimize images by:

- Choosing the right image format (e.g., JPEG, PNG, GIF) for the type of image.

- Compressing images to reduce file size without sacrificing quality.

- Using responsive images to serve different image sizes based on the user's device.

Embedding Audio and Video

HTML5 introduced native support for embedding audio and video content in web pages. You can use the `<audio>` and `<video>` elements to include media files. Here's an example:

```html
<audio controls>
  <source src="audio.mp3" type="audio/mpeg">
  Your browser does not support the audio element.
</audio>
```

- The `controls` attribute adds playback controls (play, pause, volume, etc.).

- Multiple `<source>` elements can be used to provide different formats for compatibility.

For video:

```html
<video controls>
  <source src="video.mp4" type="video/mp4">
  Your browser does not support the video element.
```

```
</video>
```

Responsive Media

With the variety of devices users use to access websites, it's important to make media content responsive. You can use CSS techniques like media queries to adjust the size and layout of media elements based on the screen size. This ensures that your images and videos look good on both desktop and mobile devices.

```css
@media screen and (max-width: 600px) {
  /* Adjust styles for smaller screens */
  img {
    max-width: 100%;
    height: auto;
  }
}
```

Accessibility Considerations

When working with media, it's crucial to consider accessibility. Provide alternative text for images (`alt` attribute) and captions or transcripts for audio and video content. This ensures that your website is usable by individuals with disabilities.

Incorporating images and media effectively can make your web pages more engaging and interactive. However, it's essential to optimize media for performance, consider responsiveness, and ensure accessibility for all users. This concludes our exploration of building interactive web pages.

CHAPTER V
Responsive Web Design

5.1 The Importance of Responsive Design

In today's digital landscape, responsive web design has become more critical than ever. With a growing variety of devices and screen sizes used to access the internet, ensuring that your website looks and functions well across all of them is essential. In this section, we'll explore the importance of responsive design, its benefits, and how to get started.

Why Responsive Design Matters

1. Improved User Experience: Responsive design ensures that your website is accessible and usable on various devices, providing a seamless and consistent experience for all users.

2. Mobile-Friendly: With the increasing use of smartphones and tablets, having a mobile-friendly website is crucial. Responsive design adapts your site's layout and content to fit smaller screens.

3. Better SEO: Search engines like Google favor mobile-friendly websites in their search rankings. A responsive design can positively impact your site's SEO performance.

4. Cost-Efficient: Maintaining a single responsive website is more cost-efficient than creating separate versions for desktop and mobile devices.

How Responsive Design Works

Responsive design uses techniques like CSS media queries and flexible layouts to adjust the appearance of a website based on the user's device. Here are some key components of responsive design:

- CSS Media Queries: Media queries allow you to apply specific CSS styles based on the characteristics of the user's device, such as screen width, height, or orientation.

```css
@media screen and (max-width: 768px) {
  /* CSS styles for screens up to 768px wide */
}
```

- Fluid Grids: Responsive layouts use flexible grids that can adapt to different screen sizes. This ensures that elements on the page resize proportionally.

- Flexible Images: Images can be made responsive by setting their maximum width to 100%. This prevents images from overflowing their container and maintains their aspect ratio.

```css
img {
  max-width: 100%;
  height: auto;
}
```

- Viewport Meta Tag: The viewport meta tag is used to control how a webpage is displayed on a mobile device. It helps in setting the initial scale and width of the viewport.

```html
<meta name="viewport" content="width=device-width, initial-scale=1.0">
```

Testing and Debugging

It's essential to test your responsive design on various devices and browsers to ensure that it works correctly. Web developer tools in modern browsers allow you to simulate different screen sizes and orientations for testing.

Conclusion

Responsive web design is not just a trend; it's a fundamental aspect of modern web development. It enables your website to reach a broader audience, provides a better user experience, and can positively impact your search engine rankings. In the following sections, we will delve deeper into the techniques and tools required to create responsive web designs.

5.2 CSS Media Queries

CSS media queries are a fundamental part of responsive web design. They allow you to apply specific CSS styles to elements based on the characteristics of the user's device, such as screen size, orientation, or resolution. In this section, we will delve into CSS media queries, how to use them effectively, and provide examples.

Understanding CSS Media Queries

Media queries use the `@media` rule to conditionally apply styles. They consist of two main parts: a media type and one or more expressions that define when the styles should be applied.

Here's the basic syntax of a media query:

```css
@media media-type and (media-feature) {
  /* CSS styles here */
}
```

- **Media Type:** Defines the type of media the styles are intended for, such as `screen` for computer screens or `print` for printed documents.

- **Media Feature:** Describes the specific condition under which the styles should be applied. Common features include `max-width`, `min-width`, `orientation`, and `resolution`.

Using Media Queries for Responsive Design

Media queries are often used to create responsive layouts by adjusting styles for different screen sizes. Let's look at a few examples:

1. Mobile-First Approach:

```css
/* Default styles for all screens */
body {
  font-size: 16px;
}

/* Media query for screens with a maximum width of 768px */
@media screen and (max-width: 768px) {
  body {
    font-size: 14px; /* Adjust font size for smaller screens */
  }
}
```

2. Desktop-First Approach:

```css
```

```css
/* Default styles for desktop screens */
body {
  font-size: 18px;
}


/* Media query for screens with a maximum width of 768px */
@media screen and (max-width: 768px) {
  body {
    font-size: 16px; /* Reduce font size for smaller screens */
  }
}
```

3. Adjusting Layout:

```css
/* Default layout styles */
.container {
  width: 100%;
}


/* Media query for screens with a minimum width of 1200px */
@media screen and (min-width: 1200px) {
```

```
.container {

  max-width: 1200px; /* Limit container width for larger screens */

  margin: 0 auto; /* Center-align the container */

 }

}
```
```

## Testing and Debugging

To test your media queries, use browser developer tools that allow you to simulate different screen sizes and orientations. It's essential to thoroughly test your responsive design on various devices to ensure it behaves as expected.

## Conclusion

CSS media queries are a powerful tool for creating responsive web designs. They enable you to adapt your site's layout and styles to different devices, improving the user experience. In the next sections, we will explore other techniques and tools for responsive web design.
```

5.3 Flexible Layouts with Flexbox

Creating flexible layouts is a crucial aspect of responsive web design. Flexbox, or the CSS Flexible Box Layout, is a powerful tool that simplifies the creation of complex layouts that adapt gracefully to various screen sizes and devices. In this section, we will explore the fundamentals of Flexbox and how to use it effectively to build responsive layouts.

Understanding Flexbox

Flexbox is a layout model that allows you to design layouts that adapt to the size of their container and the content within them. It's especially useful for arranging items within a container when their sizes are unknown or dynamic.

Here's a basic example of how Flexbox works:

```css
.container {
  display: flex;
  justify-content: center;
  align-items: center;
}
```

- `display: flex;`: This property is applied to the container element, making it a Flexbox container.

- `justify-content: center;`: This property horizontally centers the child elements within the container.

- `align-items: center;`: This property vertically centers the child elements within the container.

Creating Responsive Layouts with Flexbox

Flexbox excels at creating responsive layouts. Let's consider a common example of building a responsive navigation bar using Flexbox:

```css
/* Flex container for the navigation links */
.navbar {
  display: flex;
  justify-content: space-between; /* Distribute space evenly between items */
  align-items: center; /* Center items vertically */
}

/* Navigation links within the Flex container */
.nav-link {
  padding: 10px;
}
```

In this example, the navigation links will automatically adjust their positions and spacing based on the width of the parent container.

Flexbox Features and Properties

Flexbox offers numerous properties to control layout behavior, such as `flex-direction`, `flex-wrap`, `order`, and more. These properties allow you to create intricate and responsive designs with ease.

Testing and Browser Compatibility

Flexbox is well-supported in modern web browsers, but it's essential to test your layouts thoroughly, especially if you need to support older browsers. Tools like Autoprefixer can help ensure compatibility.

Conclusion

Flexbox is a versatile tool for creating responsive and flexible layouts in web design. Its intuitive model allows you to build complex designs while maintaining adaptability to various screen sizes. In the next sections, we will explore other techniques for responsive web design.

5.4 Creating Responsive Navigation Menus

Responsive navigation menus are a critical component of a mobile-friendly web design. They ensure that users can navigate your website comfortably, regardless of the device they're using. In this section, we will delve into the strategies for creating responsive navigation menus.

1. The Importance of Responsive Navigation Menus

Responsive navigation menus adapt to different screen sizes and orientations, making it easier for users to access your website's content. A well-designed responsive menu enhances the user experience and contributes to the overall success of your site.

2. Using CSS Media Queries

CSS media queries are the foundation of responsive design. They allow you to apply different styles and layouts based on the characteristics of the user's device. Here's an example of a media query for adjusting navigation layout at different screen sizes:

```css
/* CSS for larger screens */
@media screen and (min-width: 768px) {
  .nav-menu {
    display: flex;
    justify-content: space-between;
  }
}
```

```
/* CSS for smaller screens */
@media screen and (max-width: 767px) {
  .nav-menu {
    display: none; /* Hide the menu by default */
  }
}
```

In this example, the navigation menu switches from a horizontal layout to a hidden state on smaller screens.

3. Implementing Hamburger Menus

The hamburger menu is a common pattern for mobile navigation. It consists of a button with three horizontal lines that, when clicked, reveal the navigation links. Here's a simple HTML and CSS example:

HTML:
```html
<div class="menu-toggle">
  <div class="bar"></div>
  <div class="bar"></div>
  <div class="bar"></div>
</div>
```

```html
<ul class="nav-menu">
  <li><a href="#">Home</a></li>
  <li><a href="#">About</a></li>
  <li><a href="#">Services</a></li>
  <!-- Add more menu items here -->
</ul>
```

CSS:

```css
/* CSS for the hamburger menu icon */
.menu-toggle {
  display: block;
  cursor: pointer;
  /* Styles for the bars */
}


/* CSS for hiding the menu initially */
.nav-menu {
  display: none;
  /* Styles for the navigation links */
}
```

With this approach, clicking the hamburger menu icon reveals the navigation links, providing a mobile-friendly navigation experience.

4. Testing and Browser Compatibility

After implementing your responsive navigation, it's essential to test it on various devices and browsers. This ensures that your menu functions correctly and looks good across the board.

Conclusion

Creating responsive navigation menus is a crucial step in building a mobile-friendly website. By using CSS media queries and thoughtful design patterns like the hamburger menu, you can provide a seamless and user-friendly navigation experience on both desktop and mobile devices. In the next section, we will explore techniques for optimizing your website for mobile devices further.

5.5 Optimizing for Mobile Devices

Optimizing your website for mobile devices is a critical aspect of responsive web design. Mobile optimization ensures that your site is accessible, visually appealing, and performs well on smartphones and tablets. In this section, we will explore specific strategies for optimizing your web content for mobile devices.

1. Mobile-First Design

Mobile-first design is a fundamental concept in responsive web design. It involves creating your website with mobile devices as the primary focus and then progressively enhancing it for larger screens. Here's how to implement a mobile-first approach:

- **Start with a Simple Layout:** Begin with a clean and straightforward layout that works well on small screens. Avoid complex, multi-column designs.

- **Use Fluid Grids:** Utilize fluid grids and relative units like percentages for layout elements, allowing them to adapt to various screen sizes.

- **Prioritize Content:** Identify the most critical content and place it prominently on mobile screens. This ensures that users can access essential information without excessive scrolling or zooming.

2. Responsive Images and Media

Optimize images and media to reduce loading times and improve the mobile user experience:

- **Use the `srcset` Attribute:** The `srcset` attribute in HTML allows you to provide multiple image versions with different resolutions. Browsers can then choose the most appropriate image based on the user's device.

- **Implement Lazy Loading:** Implement lazy loading for images and videos to ensure they are only loaded when they come into the user's viewport. This reduces initial page load times.

3. Typography and Readability

Ensure that text is legible and easy to read on mobile screens:

- **Use Readable Fonts:** Choose legible fonts and maintain a consistent font size for text content.

- **Optimize Line Length:** Avoid excessively long lines of text. Use responsive typography to adjust font size and line spacing for various screen sizes.

4. Touch-Friendly Interfaces

Mobile devices rely on touch input, so make sure your website is touch-friendly:

- **Use Appropriate Touch Targets:** Buttons, links, and interactive elements should be large enough to tap accurately without accidentally activating adjacent elements.

- **Spacing and Padding:** Provide enough spacing and padding around touch elements to prevent unintended taps.

5. Performance Optimization

Mobile users often have slower internet connections, so prioritize performance:

- **Minimize HTTP Requests:** Reduce the number of HTTP requests by consolidating CSS and JavaScript files. Use browser caching to improve load times.

- **Compress Images:** Compress and optimize images to reduce file sizes while maintaining quality.

6. Test on Real Devices

Finally, thoroughly test your website on real mobile devices to ensure everything functions correctly. Emulators and testing tools can be helpful, but testing on actual smartphones and tablets is crucial for a realistic evaluation.

Conclusion

Optimizing your website for mobile devices is essential in today's mobile-centric world. By following mobile-first design principles, optimizing images and media, prioritizing readability, creating touch-friendly interfaces, and focusing on performance, you can provide an outstanding user experience for visitors on smartphones and tablets.

CHAPTER VI
Web Development Tools

6.1 Code Editors and Integrated Development Environments (IDEs)

In the world of web development, having the right tools can significantly boost your productivity and efficiency. Code editors and Integrated Development Environments (IDEs) are among the most critical tools for web developers. In this section, we'll explore the importance of choosing the right code editor or IDE and provide guidance on how to make an informed choice.

Why Choosing the Right Code Editor or IDE Matters

Your choice of a code editor or IDE impacts your workflow, code quality, and development speed. Here's why it's crucial:

1. Code Autocompletion: Code editors and IDEs offer intelligent code autocompletion, which can save you a significant amount of time by suggesting code snippets, variable names, and function names as you type.

2. Syntax Highlighting: These tools provide syntax highlighting, making it easier to spot errors and understand your code's structure.

3. Debugging Tools: Many IDEs come with built-in debugging tools that allow you to step through your code, set breakpoints, and inspect variables to find and fix issues more efficiently.

4. Integration with Version Control: Most code editors and IDEs seamlessly integrate with version control systems like Git, allowing you to track changes and collaborate with others effectively.

5. Extensibility: Many code editors and IDEs support extensions and plugins, enabling you to customize and extend their functionality according to your needs.

Choosing the Right Code Editor or IDE

The choice between a code editor and an IDE depends on your specific needs and preferences. Here are some popular options:

Code Editors:

- **Visual Studio Code (VS Code):** This free, open-source code editor from Microsoft is incredibly popular for web development. It's highly customizable, supports numerous programming languages, and offers a vast library of extensions.

- **Sublime Text:** Sublime Text is known for its speed and simplicity. It features a distraction-free interface and supports various programming languages. It's a paid tool, but you can use the evaluation version for free.

- **Atom:** Atom is another free, open-source code editor created by GitHub. It's highly customizable and has a large community of developers creating extensions and themes.

Integrated Development Environments (IDEs):

- **WebStorm:** Developed by JetBrains, WebStorm is a commercial IDE tailored specifically for web development. It offers advanced features for JavaScript, TypeScript, and HTML/CSS development.

- **Visual Studio:** Microsoft's Visual Studio IDE is a powerful tool for web development, particularly if you're working with .NET technologies. It supports various web-related languages and frameworks.

- **Eclipse:** Eclipse is a free and open-source IDE that supports web development with plugins. It's a versatile tool that can be customized to suit your needs.

Conclusion

Selecting the right code editor or IDE is a personal decision that depends on your coding preferences and project requirements. Experiment with a few options to find the one that enhances your workflow and helps you write clean, efficient code. Regardless of your choice, mastering your code editor or IDE is essential for becoming a proficient web developer.

6.2 Browser Developer Tools

Browser Developer Tools are indispensable instruments for web developers, allowing them to inspect, debug, and optimize web applications. In this section, we'll delve into the details of Browser Developer Tools, why they are essential, and how to utilize them effectively.

The Importance of Browser Developer Tools

Browser Developer Tools, commonly found in modern web browsers like Google Chrome, Mozilla Firefox, and Microsoft Edge, serve various critical purposes:

1. Debugging: Developer Tools provide a set of debugging tools that help identify and rectify issues in your web applications. You can set breakpoints, inspect variables, and step through code execution.

2. Inspecting Elements: You can inspect the structure and styles of HTML elements, making it easy to understand how a page is constructed and why certain styles are applied.

3. Network Analysis: Monitor network requests, including HTTP requests and responses. This is invaluable for optimizing page load times and diagnosing network-related issues.

4. Performance Profiling: Assess the performance of your web application to identify bottlenecks. You can analyze CPU usage, memory consumption, and rendering performance.

5. Console: Log messages and errors in the console, making it an essential tool for tracking down issues and debugging JavaScript.

Using Browser Developer Tools

Here's a step-by-step guide on how to use Browser Developer Tools effectively:

1. Opening Developer Tools: Most browsers offer Developer Tools through the context menu (right-click on a web page element and select "Inspect" or "Inspect Element") or by pressing `F12` or `Ctrl+Shift+I` (Windows/Linux) or `Cmd+Option+I` (macOS).

2. Elements Panel: The Elements panel allows you to inspect and modify the DOM structure of a web page. You can select and highlight elements, view and edit HTML and CSS, and understand the layout of a page.

3. Console Panel: The Console panel is where you can log messages and errors from your JavaScript code. Use `console.log()` to output information and troubleshoot issues.

4. Sources Panel: In the Sources panel, you can view and debug JavaScript code. Set breakpoints, step through code execution, and examine variables.

5. Network Panel: The Network panel records network activity, including HTTP requests and responses. It helps you optimize page load times and diagnose network issues.

6. Performance Panel: The Performance panel lets you record and analyze the runtime performance of your web application. It helps identify bottlenecks and slowdowns.

7. Application Panel: In this panel, you can inspect and manipulate browser storage (such as cookies, local storage, and IndexedDB) and service workers.

8. Security Panel: Check for security issues and certificate information related to the website you're inspecting.

9. Lighthouse Integration: Lighthouse is a tool integrated into some browser Developer Tools that performs audits on web pages, helping you improve performance, accessibility, SEO, and more.

Conclusion

Browser Developer Tools are your best friends when it comes to web development. They offer a rich set of features for debugging, inspecting, and optimizing web applications. By mastering these tools, you'll become a more efficient and effective web developer.

6.3 Version Control with Git and GitHub

Version control is a critical aspect of modern web development. It allows you to track changes in your codebase, collaborate with others, and maintain a history of your project. Git, along with platforms like GitHub, provides powerful version control capabilities. In this section, we will explore Git and GitHub, explaining their importance and how to use them effectively.

Understanding Version Control

Version control is a system that records changes to your files over time. It helps you track modifications, revert to previous states, and work collaboratively with others. Git is one of the most widely used version control systems.

Key Concepts in Git:

1. Repository (Repo): A repository is a directory where Git tracks changes in your project. It contains all the project's files, commit history, and configuration.

2. Commit: A commit is a snapshot of your project at a specific point in time. It represents changes made to the codebase. Each commit has a unique identifier.

3. Branch: Branches in Git allow you to work on different features or versions of your project independently. The main branch is usually called "master" or "main."

4. Clone: Cloning a repository means creating a copy of it on your local machine. You can clone repositories from platforms like GitHub.

5. Pull Request (PR): A pull request is a proposed change to a repository on GitHub. It allows collaborators to review and discuss code before merging it.

Using Git and GitHub

Here's a step-by-step guide to using Git and GitHub effectively:

1. Installation: Install Git on your local machine if it's not already installed. You can download it from the official website.

2. Configuration: Configure Git with your name and email address, which will be associated with your commits.

```bash
git config --global user.name "Your Name"
git config --global user.email "your.email@example.com"
```

3. Creating a Repository: Start a new Git repository using `git init` or clone an existing repository using `git clone`.

```bash
git init          # Create a new repository
git clone <repo-url>  # Clone an existing repository
```

4. Adding and Committing Changes: Use `git add` to stage changes and `git commit` to save them with a descriptive message.

```bash
git add .          # Stage all changes
git commit -m "Message describing the change"
```

5. Branching: Create and switch between branches using `git branch` and `git checkout`.

```bash
git branch feature   # Create a new branch
git checkout feature # Switch to the feature branch
```

6. Merging: Merge branches together using `git merge`.

```bash
git checkout main    # Switch to the main branch
git merge feature    # Merge the feature branch into main
```

7. GitHub: Sign up for a GitHub account and create a remote repository. You can push your local repository to GitHub.

```bash
git remote add origin <repo-url>  # Add the GitHub repository as a remote
git push -u origin main        # Push your code to GitHub
```

8. Collaboration: Collaborate with others by creating pull requests, reviewing code, and resolving merge conflicts.

```bash
git pull        # Fetch and merge changes from the remote repository
```

Conclusion

Version control with Git and platforms like GitHub is an integral part of modern web development. It ensures codebase stability, enables collaboration, and provides a history of changes. By mastering Git and GitHub, you can effectively manage your web development projects.

6.4 Web Development Extensions and Plugins

Web development extensions and plugins are invaluable tools that enhance the capabilities of your web browser, making it easier to build and debug websites. In this section, we will explore some of the most useful extensions and plugins available for popular web browsers like Google Chrome and Mozilla Firefox.

1. Google Chrome Extensions:

  - **Web Developer**: The Web Developer extension provides a plethora of web development tools in one package. It includes features for inspecting and editing the DOM, testing responsive designs, and disabling JavaScript, among others.

  - **Lighthouse:** Lighthouse is an extension for auditing web pages in terms of performance, accessibility, SEO, and best practices. It provides valuable insights and recommendations for improving your site.

  - **JSON Formatter:** This extension formats JSON responses in a more readable and structured way. It's helpful when working with APIs or examining JSON data.

  - **Wappalyzer:** Wappalyzer identifies the technologies used on a website, including content management systems, web frameworks, and JavaScript libraries. It's a handy tool for competitive analysis and research.

2. Mozilla Firefox Add-ons:

- Firebug: Although the Firebug extension has been deprecated, many of its features are now available in the Firefox DevTools. It allows you to inspect HTML and CSS, debug JavaScript, and monitor network activity.

- ColorZilla: ColorZilla is a color picker and gradient generator. It's useful for quickly identifying and copying colors from web pages.

- User-Agent Switcher: This extension lets you change your browser's user-agent string to test how websites behave on different devices and browsers.

- React Developer Tools: If you're working with React, this extension provides a dedicated set of tools for inspecting and debugging React components.

3. Cross-browser Extensions:

- BrowserStack: BrowserStack offers cross-browser testing directly in your browser. It allows you to test your website on various browsers and operating systems, ensuring compatibility.

- Ghostery: Ghostery helps you identify and block trackers on websites. It's useful for privacy and can also help speed up page loading times.

- LastPass: While not specific to web development, LastPass is a password manager that helps you securely manage your passwords across different sites and services.

4. Code Editors and IDEs Integrations:

- **Visual Studio Code (VS Code):** VS Code offers a vast collection of extensions for web development, including code editors for HTML, CSS, JavaScript, and various frameworks. Some popular extensions include "Live Server" for live previews and "ESLint" for code linting.

- **IntelliJ IDEA/WebStorm:** JetBrains IDEs like WebStorm provide powerful web development capabilities and integrate with popular frameworks like React and Angular. They also support version control through Git.

Conclusion:

Web development extensions and plugins significantly streamline the development process, from inspecting and debugging web pages to testing and optimizing performance. By leveraging these tools, developers can work more efficiently and produce high-quality websites. Explore the extensions and plugins that best suit your workflow to enhance your web development experience.

CHAPTER VII
Putting It All Together: Practical Projects

7.1 Project 1: Personal Portfolio Website

In this section, we will embark on an exciting journey to create your very own personal portfolio website. A personal portfolio website is a fantastic way to showcase your skills, projects, and accomplishments as a web developer. By the end of this project, you'll have a fully functional and visually appealing portfolio site to share with the world.

Project Overview:

Your personal portfolio website will serve as a digital resume and portfolio, allowing you to display your web development skills and highlight your previous projects. Here's a step-by-step guide to help you create your personal portfolio website:

Step 1: Planning and Design

  - **Define Your Goals:** Determine the purpose of your portfolio website. What do you want to achieve with it? Who is your target audience?

  - **Content Strategy:** Decide what content you want to include. This typically includes an About Me section, a portfolio showcasing your projects, a resume/CV section, and contact information.

- **Design:** Sketch the layout and design of your website. Consider the color scheme, typography, and overall aesthetics. You can use tools like Figma or Adobe XD for design mockups.

Step 2: Setting Up Your Development Environment

- **Choose a Code Editor:** Select a code editor or integrated development environment (IDE) for building your website. Popular choices include Visual Studio Code, Sublime Text, and Atom.

- **Version Control:** Set up a Git repository to track changes in your project. You can use platforms like GitHub or GitLab for remote hosting.

Step 3: Building the Website

- **HTML and CSS:** Create the structure and style of your website using HTML and CSS. Start with the homepage and work on the other sections.

- **Responsive Design:** Ensure your website is responsive, so it looks and functions well on different devices and screen sizes. Utilize CSS media queries for this purpose.

- **CSS Frameworks**: Consider using CSS frameworks like Bootstrap or Foundation to speed up development.

Step 4: Adding Functionality

- **JavaScript:** Enhance your website with interactivity using JavaScript. You can create animations, add form validation, or implement smooth scrolling, among other features.

- **Contact Form:** Implement a contact form to allow visitors to get in touch with you. You may use server-side technologies like Node.js or PHP to handle form submissions.

Step 5: Testing and Debugging

- **Cross-Browser Testing:** Ensure your website works correctly on various web browsers (Chrome, Firefox, Safari, Edge).

- **Testing on Mobile Devices:** Verify that your website is mobile-friendly and functions well on smartphones and tablets.

Step 6: Deployment

- **Web Hosting:** Choose a web hosting service to deploy your portfolio. Popular options include Netlify, Vercel, GitHub Pages, or traditional web hosts.

- **Domain Name:** Consider registering a custom domain name for your portfolio (e.g., www.yourname.com).

Step 7: Optimization

- **Performance Optimization:** Optimize your website's images, CSS, and JavaScript to ensure fast loading times.

- **SEO Optimization:** Implement basic SEO practices to make your portfolio more discoverable on search engines.

Step 8: Maintenance and Updates

- **Regular Updates:** Keep your portfolio up-to-date with your latest projects and accomplishments.

- **Security:** Ensure your website is secure by keeping software and plugins up-to-date.

By the end of this project, you'll have not only a stunning personal portfolio website but also a deep understanding of web development principles and practices. Your portfolio will be a reflection of your skills and a valuable tool in your career as a web developer. Good luck, and enjoy the journey of creating your online presence!

7.2 Project 2: Interactive Photo Gallery

In this section, we'll dive into the creation of an interactive photo gallery—a web application that allows users to view and interact with a collection of images. This project will not only enhance your web development skills but also add an engaging feature to your web development portfolio.

Project Overview:

An interactive photo gallery typically includes features like displaying images in a grid or carousel, allowing users to click on images for a closer view, and providing navigation options. Below is a step-by-step guide on how to create this project:

Step 1: Planning and Design

  - **Project Scope:** Define the scope of your interactive photo gallery. Determine the number of images you want to showcase and any specific features you'd like to implement, such as image captions or categories.

  - **Design:** Plan the layout and design of your gallery. Consider using tools like Figma or Adobe XD to create design mockups. Ensure the design is user-friendly and visually appealing.

Step 2: Setting Up Your Development Environment

  - **Code Editor:** Choose a code editor or integrated development environment (IDE) for coding. Popular options include Visual Studio Code, Sublime Text, and Atom.

- **Version Control:** Set up a Git repository to track changes in your project. Platforms like GitHub or GitLab can host your remote repository.

Step 3: Building the Photo Gallery

- **HTML and CSS:** Create the structure of your photo gallery using HTML and apply CSS to style it. Begin with a grid layout to display the images.

- **Image Assets:** Prepare and optimize the images you want to showcase in your gallery. Consider using image compression tools to reduce file sizes.

Step 4: Adding Functionality

- **JavaScript:** Enhance your gallery's interactivity using JavaScript. Implement features such as image pop-ups (lightbox effect), navigation arrows, and image captions.

- **Lightbox Library:** You can use existing JavaScript libraries like Lightbox2 or create your custom lightbox functionality.

Step 5: User Experience Enhancements

- **Responsive Design:** Ensure your photo gallery is responsive, adapting to various screen sizes and devices.

- **Keyboard Navigation:** Allow users to navigate the gallery using keyboard arrow keys for accessibility.

Step 6: Testing and Debugging

- **Cross-Browser Testing:** Test your gallery on different web browsers (Chrome, Firefox, Safari, Edge) to ensure consistent functionality.

- **Performance Testing:** Optimize your gallery for fast loading times by minimizing JavaScript and CSS file sizes.

Step 7: Deployment

- **Web Hosting:** Choose a web hosting service to deploy your interactive photo gallery. Services like Netlify, Vercel, and GitHub Pages are suitable for hosting static sites.

- **Domain Name:** Consider registering a custom domain name for your gallery (e.g., www.yourgallery.com).

Step 8: Optimization and Maintenance

- **Performance Optimization:** Continuously optimize your gallery for faster loading times by optimizing images and code.

- **Updates:** Keep your gallery up-to-date with new images or features.

Creating an interactive photo gallery is a great way to demonstrate your skills in web development, user experience design, and project planning. By the end of this project, you'll have a fully functional and visually appealing photo gallery to showcase your work or personal interests. Enjoy the process of bringing images to life on the web!

7.3 Project 3: Contact Form with Server-Side Integration

In this section, we will embark on the journey of creating a Contact Form with Server-Side Integration. This project will teach you how to design a functional contact form on your website, capture user inputs, and send them to a server for processing. By the end of this project, you will have a valuable skill set for building interactive forms and integrating server-side processing.

Project Overview:

A contact form is a vital component for websites, allowing users to reach out to you or your organization conveniently. Here are the steps to create a contact form with server-side integration:

Step 1: Planning and Design

  - **Project Scope:** Determine the key information you want to collect from users through the contact form. Common fields include name, email, subject, and message.

  - **Design:** Plan the layout and design of your contact form. Ensure it is user-friendly and visually matches the aesthetics of your website.

Step 2: Setting Up Your Development Environment

  - **Code Editor:** Choose a code editor or integrated development environment (IDE) for coding. Popular options include Visual Studio Code, Sublime Text, and Atom.

- Server-Side Technology: Select a server-side technology for handling form submissions. Common options include PHP, Node.js, Python (Django or Flask), or Ruby on Rails.

Step 3: Building the Contact Form (Frontend)

- HTML: Create the HTML structure of your contact form, including input fields, labels, and a submit button.

- CSS: Style your form to match your website's design, making it visually appealing and responsive.

Step 4: Capturing User Inputs (Frontend)

- JavaScript: Implement JavaScript to capture user inputs and perform basic client-side validation. Ensure that required fields are filled out correctly.

Step 5: Server-Side Integration

- Backend Script: Write the server-side script to process form submissions. This script will receive data from the frontend, validate it, and send an email or store it in a database.

- Security: Implement security measures to prevent common vulnerabilities, such as cross-site scripting (XSS) and SQL injection.

Step 6: Form Submission Handling

- Validation: Validate user inputs on the server-side to ensure data integrity and security.

- **Email Notifications:** Set up email notifications to receive contact form submissions in your inbox.

Step 7: Success and Error Handling

- **Success Page:** Create a success page that users are redirected to after successfully submitting the form.

- **Error Handling:** Implement error handling to display meaningful error messages when form submissions fail.

Step 8: Testing and Debugging

- **Testing:** Test your contact form thoroughly. Check for edge cases and ensure all validation and error messages work as expected.

- **Cross-Browser Testing:** Ensure that your form functions correctly on various web browsers.

Step 9: Deployment

- **Server Hosting:** Deploy your website and server-side scripts to a web hosting provider that supports your chosen server-side technology.

- **Domain Name:** Consider registering a custom domain name for your website if you haven't already.

Step 10: Post-Deployment Maintenance

- **Monitoring:** Monitor form submissions and server performance.

- **Updates:** Regularly update your website and server-side scripts to address security and functionality improvements.

Creating a contact form with server-side integration is an essential skill for web developers. It enables you to connect with your website's users and receive their inquiries or feedback efficiently. By following the steps outlined in this project, you'll have a functional and secure contact form integrated into your website. Enjoy enhancing your web development portfolio with this valuable project!

CHAPTER VIII
Web Hosting and Deployment

8.1 Choosing a Domain Name

Choosing the right domain name for your website is a crucial step in establishing your online presence. A domain name is the web address that users will type into their browsers to access your site. Here, we'll discuss the details of choosing a domain name and the considerations you should keep in mind.

Understanding Domain Names:

A domain name consists of two main parts:

1. Domain Name itself: This is the unique name that identifies your website. For example, in "example.com," "example" is the domain name.

2. Top-Level Domain (TLD): This is the suffix that follows the domain name. Common TLDs include .com, .org, .net, .edu, .gov, and many others.

Tips for Choosing a Domain Name:

1. Relevance: Your domain name should reflect the purpose or content of your website. It should give users an idea of what to expect when they visit.

2. Short and Memorable: Shorter domain names are easier to remember and type. Avoid long or complex names that users might mistype.

3. Avoid Special Characters and Numbers: Stick to letters to avoid confusion. Hyphens can be used if necessary, but they should be used sparingly.

4. Keyword Research: If your website has a specific niche or target audience, consider including relevant keywords in your domain name. This can help with search engine optimization (SEO).

5. Brandable: A domain name can be a brand asset. Choose a name that is unique and can be associated with your brand.

6. Check Availability: Use domain registrar websites or tools to check if your desired domain name is available. If it's not, you may need to get creative or consider alternative TLDs.

Domain Registrar:

To register a domain name, you'll need to use a domain registrar. Popular domain registrars include:

- **GoDaddy**

- **Namecheap**

- **Google Domains**

- **HostGator**

- **Bluehost**

Pricing:

The cost of domain registration can vary depending on the domain registrar and the chosen TLD. Prices typically range from a few dollars per year to more premium prices for certain TLDs.

Domain Privacy:

Consider opting for domain privacy protection, sometimes called WHOIS privacy. This service keeps your personal contact information associated with the domain name private and replaces it with the registrar's contact information.

Renewal Fees:

Be aware of domain renewal fees. Domain registration is typically an annual cost, and failure to renew can result in losing your domain.

Legal Considerations:

Ensure that your chosen domain name doesn't infringe on any trademarks or copyrights. It's essential to respect the intellectual property rights of others.

Conclusion:

Choosing a domain name is a significant decision for your website. It's the first impression users will have of your online presence. Take your time, consider your website's purpose, and choose a name that represents your brand or content effectively. Once you've selected the perfect domain name, you'll be ready to move on to the next steps in web hosting and deployment.

8.2 Selecting a Web Hosting Provider

Choosing the right web hosting provider is a crucial decision when it comes to getting your website online. A web hosting provider is a company that stores your website files and makes them accessible on the internet. In this section, we'll dive into the details of selecting the right web hosting provider for your needs.

Types of Web Hosting:

Before we get into the selection process, it's essential to understand the various types of web hosting available. The most common types include:

1. Shared Hosting: Your website shares server resources with other websites on the same server. It's a cost-effective option suitable for small websites and beginners.

2. Virtual Private Server (VPS) Hosting: VPS hosting offers a dedicated portion of a server's resources. It's more robust and allows for greater customization.

3. Dedicated Hosting: With dedicated hosting, you have an entire server to yourself, providing maximum performance and control. It's suitable for large websites with high traffic.

4. Cloud Hosting: Cloud hosting uses a network of virtual servers, allowing for scalability and flexibility. You only pay for the resources you use.

Key Factors When Selecting a Web Hosting Provider:

1. Reliability and Uptime: Look for providers with a strong track record of uptime (the time your website is accessible). Reliability is crucial to ensure your site is always available to users.

2. Performance: Fast loading times are essential for user experience and SEO. Evaluate the provider's server performance and location.

3. Scalability: Consider your website's potential for growth. A good hosting provider should offer scalability options as your site expands.

4. Customer Support: Access to reliable customer support is critical, especially in case of technical issues. Look for providers with responsive support teams.

5. Security: Hosting providers should offer security features like SSL certificates, regular backups, and firewall protection to keep your website safe.

6. Control Panel: A user-friendly control panel (e.g., cPanel or Plesk) simplifies server management tasks.

7. Pricing and Plans: Compare hosting plans and pricing to find one that fits your budget. Be aware of any hidden fees or renewal costs.

8. Reviews and Recommendations: Read reviews and seek recommendations from other website owners to gauge user experiences with specific hosting providers.

9. Data Center Locations: Consider the geographical location of the provider's data centers. Choosing a data center closer to your target audience can improve website speed.

Popular Web Hosting Providers:

Here are some well-known web hosting providers to consider:

- **Bluehost**

- **HostGator**

- **SiteGround**

- **A2 Hosting**

- **InMotion Hosting**

- **DreamHost**

Conclusion:

Selecting the right web hosting provider is a critical step in launching your website. Consider your specific needs, budget, and growth plans when making your decision. Once you've chosen a provider, you can move on to the next steps in web hosting and deployment, such as uploading your website, testing, troubleshooting, and finally, launching your site for the world to see.

8.3 Uploading Your Website

Once you've chosen a domain name and a web hosting provider, the next crucial step is to upload your website to the hosting server. This process involves transferring your website's files, databases, and other assets to a location where they can be publicly accessed on the internet. In this section, we'll walk you through the steps to upload your website effectively.

1. Prepare Your Website Files:

Before you start the upload process, make sure you have all the necessary website files ready. This typically includes HTML, CSS, JavaScript files, images, and any other assets required for your site.

2. Choose an Upload Method:

There are several methods to upload your website files to your hosting server:

   - File Transfer Protocol (FTP): FTP is a standard method for uploading files to a web server. You'll need FTP client software (e.g., FileZilla, Cyberduck) to connect to your server and transfer files.

   - Control Panel File Manager: Many hosting providers offer a web-based file manager in their control panel (e.g., cPanel or Plesk). You can use this tool to upload files directly from your browser.

   - Git and Version Control: If you're using version control systems like Git, you can push your code to a remote repository on your server and then pull it to deploy.

3. Access Your Hosting Account:

Log in to your hosting account using the credentials provided by your hosting provider. You'll typically receive an FTP username and password or access to a control panel.

4. Configure FTP Client:

If you're using FTP, configure your FTP client with the server's hostname, your username, password, and port (usually 21 for FTP or 22 for SFTP). Connect to the server.

5. Navigate to the Website Root Directory:

Once connected, navigate to the root directory where your website should be stored. This is often named "public_html" or "www."

6. Upload Your Website:

Now, you can upload your website files to the server. You can either drag and drop files using the FTP client or use the control panel's file manager to upload them.

7. Test Your Website:

After the upload is complete, it's essential to test your website to ensure everything works as expected. Check for broken links, missing assets, and any issues with your website's functionality.

8. Configure Databases and Settings:

If your website relies on databases, make sure to configure them correctly. Update any configuration files (e.g., database connection settings) to reflect your hosting environment.

9. DNS and Domain Configuration:

If you've just registered a new domain or changed DNS settings, you may need to wait for DNS propagation, which can take up to 48 hours. During this time, your website might not be accessible from all locations.

10. Monitor and Troubleshoot:

Regularly monitor your website for any issues. Use tools like website uptime monitoring services to ensure your site is accessible.

Conclusion:

Uploading your website to a hosting server is a fundamental step in making it accessible on the internet. By following the steps outlined above and testing your website thoroughly, you'll ensure a smooth deployment process. Once your site is successfully uploaded and tested, you can move on to the final step of launching your website for the world to see.

8.4 Testing and Troubleshooting

After you've uploaded your website and before you officially launch it to the public, it's crucial to thoroughly test and troubleshoot your site to ensure it functions correctly and provides an excellent user experience. In this section, we'll guide you through the testing and troubleshooting process.

1. Functional Testing:

Start by conducting functional testing to check if all the website's features and functionalities are working as expected. Test various scenarios and user interactions, such as:

- Navigating through the website's pages.

- Filling out and submitting forms.

- Interacting with interactive elements (e.g., buttons, sliders).

- Testing any user authentication or login systems.

2. Cross-Browser Compatibility:

Test your website in different web browsers (e.g., Chrome, Firefox, Safari, Edge) to ensure it appears and functions correctly on all major platforms. Pay special attention to older browser versions, as they may have compatibility issues.

3. Responsiveness:

Test your website's responsiveness by checking how it appears on various devices, including desktops, laptops, tablets, and smartphones. Ensure that the content adjusts appropriately to different screen sizes.

4. Performance Testing:

Website speed is critical for user satisfaction and search engine rankings. Use tools like Google PageSpeed Insights or GTmetrix to analyze your website's performance and identify areas for improvement.

5. SEO and Metadata:

Verify that your website has proper meta titles, descriptions, and structured data. Ensure that URLs are SEO-friendly, and check for broken links or 404 errors.

6. Security Testing:

Security is paramount. Scan your website for vulnerabilities using tools like OWASP ZAP or security plugins if you're using a CMS like WordPress. Make sure your SSL certificate is correctly installed for secure connections (HTTPS).

7. Content Review:

Review all content for accuracy and correctness. Check for typos, grammatical errors, and outdated information. Ensure that all images and multimedia assets load correctly.

8. Forms and User Data:

If your website collects user data through forms, test the data submission process and make sure user information is captured correctly and securely.

9. Accessibility:

Ensure your website is accessible to all users, including those with disabilities. Test for compliance with WCAG (Web Content Accessibility Guidelines) standards.

10. Cross-Device Testing:

Test your website on various devices and operating systems to verify consistent performance and appearance.

Troubleshooting:

During testing, you may encounter issues. Here's a troubleshooting process:

- Identify the problem: Isolate and understand the issue. Use browser developer tools and error messages to pinpoint the problem's source.

- Fix the issue: Once you've identified the problem, take corrective action. This might involve adjusting code, updating configurations, or fixing broken links.

- Retest: After making changes, retest your website to ensure the issue has been resolved.

- Document changes: Keep a record of changes made during troubleshooting for future reference.

Conclusion:

Thoroughly testing and troubleshooting your website before launching it is crucial to provide a seamless user experience and avoid potential issues. Regularly revisit your testing process as you make updates and additions to your site to maintain its quality and functionality. Once you're confident that your website is error-free and fully functional, you can proceed to the final step: launching your website for the world to see.

8.5 Launching Your Website

Congratulations! You've gone through the process of building your website, choosing a domain name, selecting a web hosting provider, uploading your content, and testing it thoroughly. Now it's time to launch your website and make it accessible to the world. Here's a step-by-step guide on how to do it:

1. Final Testing:

Before launching, perform one last round of testing to ensure everything is working correctly. Double-check links, forms, images, and functionality. Make sure there are no errors or issues.

2. Backups:

Take a full backup of your website, including databases and files. This is a precautionary step in case anything goes wrong during the launch.

3. DNS Configuration:

If you've registered your domain name separately from your hosting provider, you'll need to configure the Domain Name System (DNS) settings. Update your domain's DNS records to point to your web hosting server. This step may take some time to propagate across the internet, so be patient.

4. SSL Certificate:

Ensure that your SSL certificate is correctly configured and active, especially if you're using HTTPS for a secure connection. Visitors should see the padlock icon in their browser's address bar, indicating a secure site.

5. Robots.txt and Sitemap:

Check your website's `robots.txt` file to ensure that search engines can crawl your site. Submit your sitemap to search engines like Google to improve indexing.

6. Remove Maintenance Pages:

If you had a "Coming Soon" or "Under Maintenance" page on your website, remove it to make your site publicly accessible.

7. Load Testing:

Consider running load tests if you expect a significant amount of traffic upon launch. This helps ensure your website can handle high traffic loads.

8. Monitor and Analytics:

Set up website monitoring and analytics tools to track your site's performance and user interactions. Google Analytics is a popular choice for this purpose.

9. Social Media and SEO:

Share your website on social media platforms and optimize it for search engines. Use proper meta titles, descriptions, and keywords to improve visibility.

10. Launch Announcement:

Consider making an announcement or blog post about your website's launch. Share it with your existing audience or subscribers.

11. Launch!

Once everything is in order, it's time to launch your website. Update your DNS records if necessary and point your domain to your hosting provider. This process may take a few hours to a couple of days to fully propagate.

12. Monitor and Support:

After the launch, monitor your website closely for any issues. Be prepared to provide support and address any user feedback or problems that arise.

13. Post-Launch SEO and Marketing:

Continue to optimize your website for search engines and engage in marketing efforts to attract visitors and grow your online presence.

Conclusion:

Launching your website is an exciting step in your web development journey. By following these steps and ensuring everything is in order, you can ensure a smooth and successful launch. Remember that maintaining your website, updating content, and regularly checking for issues are ongoing responsibilities as a website owner.

CHAPTER IX
Web Development Best Practices

9.1 Writing Clean and Maintainable Code

Writing clean and maintainable code is crucial for the long-term success of your web development projects. Clean code is easier to read, debug, and extend, making it more efficient and cost-effective in the long run. Here's a comprehensive guide on how to write clean and maintainable code:

1. Meaningful Variable and Function Names:

Choose descriptive names for variables, functions, and classes. Aim for clarity and readability so that anyone reading your code can understand its purpose without extensive comments.

```javascript
// Not recommended

let x = 5; // What does x represent?


// Recommended

let numberOfUsers = 5; // Clearly defines the variable's purpose
```

2. Consistent Code Style:

Adopt a consistent code style, including indentation, spacing, and naming conventions. Use linters and code formatting tools like ESLint and Prettier to automate style checks.

3. Comments and Documentation:

Include comments for complex logic, explaining why certain decisions were made. Write clear and concise documentation for your functions, classes, and APIs using tools like JSDoc.

```javascript
/
 * Calculates the sum of two numbers.
 * @param {number} a - The first number.
 * @param {number} b - The second number.
 * @returns {number} The sum of a and b.
 */
function add(a, b) {
  return a + b;
}
```

4. Break Code into Functions:

Keep functions and methods small and focused on specific tasks. Avoid monolithic functions that perform multiple actions. This enhances readability and testability.

5. Avoid Global Variables:

Minimize the use of global variables, as they can lead to unexpected side effects and make debugging difficult. Use module patterns or ES6 modules to encapsulate code.

6. Error Handling:

Implement proper error handling with try-catch blocks or error-handling middleware. Provide meaningful error messages to assist in debugging.

7. Version Control:

Use version control systems like Git to track changes in your codebase. Commit regularly with descriptive commit messages. Branch your code for new features or bug fixes.

8. Code Reviews:

Encourage code reviews among team members to catch issues early and ensure adherence to coding standards. Code review tools like GitHub Pull Requests can be beneficial.

9. Testing:

Write unit tests and integration tests to validate your code's functionality. Test-driven development (TDD) can help you write cleaner and more maintainable code.

10. Refactoring:

Regularly review and refactor your code to eliminate redundancy, improve efficiency, and adhere to evolving best practices. Refactoring tools and patterns can assist in this process.

11. Performance Considerations:

Optimize code for performance, but maintain a balance between performance and readability. Profile your code to identify bottlenecks and address them selectively.

12. Stay Informed:

Keep up with web development trends, best practices, and emerging technologies. Attend conferences, read blogs, and participate in online communities to stay informed.

Conclusion:

Writing clean and maintainable code is a skill that every web developer should prioritize. It not only improves collaboration within a development team but also ensures that your projects remain scalable, adaptable, and easy to maintain in the long term. Consistently applying these best practices will help you become a more efficient and effective web developer.

9.2 Performance Optimization

Performance optimization is a critical aspect of web development. It ensures that your web applications load quickly and run smoothly, providing a better user experience. In this section, we'll explore various techniques and best practices for optimizing the performance of your web applications.

1. Minify and Bundle Assets:

Reduce the size of your HTML, CSS, and JavaScript files by minifying them. Minification removes unnecessary whitespace and renames variables to shorter names without altering functionality. Bundling combines multiple files into one, reducing the number of requests made to the server.

2. Optimize Images:

Optimize images for the web by compressing them and using modern image formats like WebP. Consider responsive images that load different sizes based on the user's device and screen size.

3. Use Content Delivery Networks (CDNs):

Leverage CDNs to distribute your assets across multiple servers located worldwide. CDNs can deliver assets faster to users by serving them from a server geographically closer to the user's location.

4. Lazy Loading:

Implement lazy loading for images and other non-essential resources. This technique delays the loading of offscreen content until the user scrolls to it, reducing initial page load times.

5. Minimize HTTP Requests:

Minimize the number of HTTP requests made by reducing the number of external resources (CSS, JavaScript, fonts, etc.) and using CSS sprites for small images.

6. Browser Caching:

Leverage browser caching by setting appropriate cache headers for your assets. Cached resources are stored on the user's device and can be reused for subsequent visits, reducing the need to download them again.

7. Server-Side Rendering (SSR):

Consider server-side rendering for single-page applications (SPAs) to improve initial load times and SEO. SSR generates HTML on the server before sending it to the client, reducing client-side rendering overhead.

8. Database Optimization:

Optimize database queries and indexes to improve the efficiency of data retrieval and storage. Use tools like database profilers and query optimizers to identify bottlenecks.

9. Code Splitting:

Implement code splitting to load only the necessary JavaScript code for each page. This reduces the initial bundle size and speeds up page load times.

10. Performance Monitoring:

Regularly monitor your application's performance using tools like Google Lighthouse, WebPageTest, or browser developer tools. Identify and address performance bottlenecks as they arise.

11. Responsive Design:

Ensure that your web design is responsive, so content adapts to different screen sizes and devices. A well-designed responsive layout can improve perceived performance.

12. Prioritize Above-the-Fold Content:

Load critical content above the fold (visible portion of the page) first to give users the impression of a faster page load. Lazy-load non-critical content below the fold.

13. Content Delivery Optimization:

Optimize the way you deliver content by using HTTP/2 or HTTP/3 for faster loading and reduced latency. Also, consider serverless architecture for scalability.

14. Reduce Third-Party Scripts:

Limit the use of third-party scripts and services, as they can significantly impact performance. Evaluate their necessity and consider async or deferred loading.

15. Compression:

Enable server-level compression (e.g., GZIP or Brotli) to reduce the size of data transferred over the network.

By implementing these performance optimization techniques, you can significantly enhance the speed and efficiency of your web applications. Remember that performance is an ongoing process, and continuous monitoring and improvement are essential to provide the best user experience.

9.3 Web Security Basics

Web security is of paramount importance in today's digital landscape. As a web developer, you must be aware of potential threats and take steps to protect your applications and users. This section covers fundamental web security practices to help safeguard your web projects.

1. Input Validation:

Always validate user inputs to prevent common attacks like SQL injection and Cross-Site Scripting (XSS). Use server-side validation to ensure that data submitted by users is safe and within the expected format.

2. Cross-Origin Resource Sharing (CORS):

Implement proper CORS policies to control which domains can access resources on your server. This prevents unauthorized domains from making requests to your server.

3. HTTPS (SSL/TLS):

Secure your web applications by enabling HTTPS through SSL/TLS certificates. This ensures that data transmitted between the user's browser and your server is encrypted and protected from eavesdropping.

4. Authentication and Authorization:

Implement strong user authentication and authorization mechanisms. Use techniques like password hashing and token-based authentication to secure user accounts and protect sensitive data.

5. Security Headers:

Utilize security headers like Content Security Policy (CSP), X-Content-Type-Options, X-Frame-Options, and X-XSS-Protection to mitigate various security risks. These headers provide an extra layer of defense against common web vulnerabilities.

6. Rate Limiting and DDoS Protection:

Implement rate limiting to prevent abuse of your APIs and services. Consider Distributed Denial of Service (DDoS) protection services to safeguard against large-scale attacks.

7. Error Handling:

Handle errors gracefully, but avoid revealing sensitive information to users. Customize error messages to avoid exposing internal system details.

8. Security Libraries and Frameworks:

Leverage security libraries and frameworks designed for your programming language or framework. These tools can help you implement best practices and avoid common security pitfalls.

9. Regular Updates:

Keep all software components, including your web server, database, and third-party libraries, up to date. Vulnerabilities can arise over time, and updates often contain security patches.

10. Security Audits and Penetration Testing:

Regularly conduct security audits and penetration testing to identify vulnerabilities in your application. Address any issues discovered during these assessments promptly.

11. Cross-Site Request Forgery (CSRF) Protection:

Implement CSRF protection mechanisms to prevent attackers from tricking users into performing actions they didn't intend to on your website.

12. Data Encryption:

Encrypt sensitive data at rest, such as user passwords and payment information, using strong encryption algorithms.

13. Privacy Considerations:

Respect user privacy by following data protection regulations like GDPR (General Data Protection Regulation) and implementing privacy-focused features.

14. Content Security Policy (CSP):

Use CSP headers to control which resources can be loaded by your web pages. This helps mitigate risks related to unauthorized script execution.

15. Security Education:

Educate your development team about security best practices and encourage a security-conscious culture.

By adhering to these web security basics, you can significantly reduce the risk of security breaches and protect both your applications and your users' data. Remember that security is an ongoing process, and staying informed about emerging threats and best practices is crucial.

9.4 Accessibility Guidelines

Accessibility in web development refers to creating web content and applications that can be accessed and used by everyone, including individuals with disabilities. Ensuring your web projects are accessible is not just a good practice; it's often a legal requirement. Here are some guidelines and best practices for making your websites and web applications more accessible:

1. Semantic HTML:

Use semantic HTML elements like `<header>`, `<nav>`, `<main>`, `<section>`, `<article>`, and `<footer>` to give your web pages a clear structure. Screen readers and other assistive technologies rely on semantic HTML to understand and present content properly.

2. Alt Text for Images:

Always provide descriptive `alt` text for images. This is essential for users who rely on screen readers, as it conveys the content and purpose of images.

```html
<img src="image.jpg" alt="A person using a laptop computer">
```

3. Keyboard Navigation:

Ensure that all interactive elements on your website can be accessed and used with a keyboard. Test your site's keyboard navigation and focus order to make sure it's logical and intuitive.

4. ARIA Roles and Attributes:

Use ARIA (Accessible Rich Internet Applications) roles and attributes to enhance the accessibility of dynamic web content, such as web applications. ARIA can help convey information to assistive technologies about how elements behave and should be interacted with.

5. Color Contrast:

Maintain sufficient color contrast between text and background colors to ensure readability for users with visual impairments. There are online tools available to check color contrast ratios.

6. Testing with Assistive Technologies:

Test your website or web application with screen readers, voice recognition software, and other assistive technologies. This will help you identify and fix accessibility issues.

7. Keyboard Focus Styles:

Provide visible and clear focus styles for interactive elements like links and buttons. Users should be able to see which element is currently in focus when navigating your site with a keyboard.

8. Captions and Transcripts:

For multimedia content like videos and podcasts, provide captions and transcripts. This benefits users who are deaf or hard of hearing and also makes your content more searchable.

9. Consistent and Predictable Navigation:

Keep navigation menus and layouts consistent across your site. Users should be able to predict where to find content and features.

10. Skip to Content Links:

Include "Skip to content" links at the beginning of each page to allow keyboard users to jump directly to the main content, bypassing repetitive navigation menus.

11. Document Structure:

Ensure a logical document structure with headings (h1, h2, h3, etc.) that reflect the content hierarchy. Screen readers use these headings to help users understand the page's structure.

12. User Testing:

Engage users with disabilities for usability testing. They can provide valuable feedback on the accessibility of your site and help you identify areas for improvement.

13. Stay Informed:

Web accessibility guidelines and best practices evolve. Stay informed about updates to accessibility standards, and be prepared to adapt your projects accordingly.

By following these accessibility guidelines, you can make your web projects more inclusive and ensure that everyone, regardless of their abilities, can access and use your content and applications. This not only benefits users but also helps you reach a wider audience and remain compliant with accessibility regulations.

9.5 Keeping Up with Web Development Trends

In the ever-evolving world of web development, staying up-to-date with the latest trends and technologies is essential to remain competitive and deliver high-quality web projects. Here are some strategies to help you keep up with web development trends:

1. Continuous Learning:

Web development is a field that continually changes and evolves. Dedicate time to continuous learning. This can include online courses, tutorials, webinars, or attending conferences and workshops.

2. Follow Industry Blogs and News:

Subscribe to web development blogs, news websites, and newsletters. Some popular resources include Smashing Magazine, CSS-Tricks, and A List Apart. These sources often feature articles on the latest trends and best practices.

3. Online Communities:

Join online developer communities, forums, and social media groups. Websites like Stack Overflow, GitHub, and Reddit have active developer communities where you can ask questions, share knowledge, and stay updated.

4. GitHub Trends:

GitHub's "Trending" section is an excellent place to discover new and popular web development projects, libraries, and frameworks. This can give you insights into what technologies are gaining traction.

5. Experiment and Build Projects:

Hands-on experience is one of the best ways to learn. Experiment with new technologies by building personal projects. This allows you to gain practical experience and a deeper understanding of emerging tools and frameworks.

6. Attend Meetups and Conferences:

If possible, attend local meetups, conferences, and workshops related to web development. These events provide opportunities to network with peers and learn from experts in the field.

7. Follow Thought Leaders:

Identify thought leaders in web development and follow them on social media platforms like Twitter and LinkedIn. They often share insights, news, and articles related to the latest trends.

8. Online Courses and Certifications:

Consider enrolling in online courses and certification programs that focus on specific web development technologies and trends. Platforms like Coursera, edX, and Udemy offer a wide range of courses.

9. Keep an Eye on Emerging Technologies:

Stay informed about emerging technologies such as Progressive Web Apps (PWAs), WebAssembly, and WebVR/AR. Understanding these technologies can give you a competitive edge.

10. Read Books:

While online resources are valuable, don't underestimate the depth of knowledge found in books. There are many web development books that dive deep into specific topics and technologies.

11. Collaborate on Open Source Projects:

Contributing to open-source projects can help you gain experience with cutting-edge technologies and collaborate with developers worldwide. GitHub is a great platform for finding open-source projects to contribute to.

12. Set Learning Goals:

Establish clear learning goals for yourself. Whether it's mastering a new JavaScript framework or becoming proficient in a particular programming language, having defined objectives will keep you motivated.

13. Reflect and Adapt:

Periodically review your skills and knowledge. Are there areas where you need improvement? Are there trends you've overlooked? Be open to adapting your learning path based on your assessments.

Remember that staying updated with web development trends is an ongoing process. By investing time and effort into continuous learning and exploration, you'll be well-prepared to tackle new challenges and deliver innovative web projects that meet the demands of the ever-changing digital landscape.

CHAPTER X
Beyond the Basics: What's Next?

10.1 Exploring Advanced JavaScript and Frameworks

As you progress in your web development journey, you'll encounter opportunities to delve into advanced JavaScript concepts and explore powerful frameworks that can significantly enhance your web development capabilities. In this section, we will explore some of these advanced topics.

1. Advanced JavaScript Concepts:

  - **Closures and Scopes:** Deepen your understanding of closures and how they can be used to manage variable scope in your applications.

  - **Promises and Async/Await:** Learn how to work with asynchronous code using promises and the more recent async/await syntax, making it easier to manage asynchronous operations.

  - **Higher-Order Functions:** Understand the concept of higher-order functions and how they can simplify complex operations in your code.

  - **Design Patterns:** Explore common design patterns in JavaScript, such as the Singleton, Factory, and Module patterns, to write more maintainable and scalable code.

2. JavaScript Frameworks:

   - **React:** Dive into React, a popular JavaScript library for building user interfaces. Learn about components, state management, and how to create interactive and dynamic web applications.

   - **Angular:** Explore the Angular framework, a comprehensive solution for building web applications. Understand concepts like modules, components, and services.

   - **Vue.js:** Discover Vue.js, a progressive JavaScript framework for building user interfaces. Learn about Vue components, directives, and state management.

3. Advanced Frontend Development:

   - **State Management:** Explore state management libraries like Redux (for React) or Vuex (for Vue.js) to efficiently manage application state.

   - **Routing:** Learn how to implement client-side routing using libraries like React Router or Vue Router to create single-page applications.

   - **Webpack:** Understand Webpack, a popular module bundler, and task runner for JavaScript applications. It's essential for optimizing and bundling your code.

4. Backend Development and Server-Side Programming:

   - **Node.js:** Delve into server-side JavaScript development using Node.js. Learn to build APIs, work with databases, and create server applications.

- **Express.js:** Explore Express.js, a web application framework for Node.js, which simplifies building robust, scalable APIs and web applications.

5. API Integration and Databases:

- **RESTful APIs:** Learn how to consume and create RESTful APIs, enabling your applications to interact with external services and data sources.

- **Database Integration:** Explore databases like MySQL, PostgreSQL, or NoSQL databases like MongoDB. Understand data modeling, queries, and database management.

6. Building Web Applications:

- **Full-Stack Development:** Combine your frontend and backend skills to become a full-stack developer capable of building entire web applications from scratch.

- **Authentication and Authorization:** Implement user authentication and authorization to secure your web applications.

7. Performance and Optimization:

- **Performance Tuning:** Learn strategies for optimizing the performance of your web applications, including code splitting, lazy loading, and reducing bundle sizes.

- **Progressive Web Apps (PWAs):** Explore the concept of PWAs, which are web applications that provide an app-like experience, including offline capabilities and push notifications.

8. Emerging Technologies:

- **WebAssembly:** Get a glimpse of WebAssembly, a binary instruction format that allows high-performance execution of code on web browsers.

- **WebXR:** Discover WebXR, which enables augmented and virtual reality experiences within web applications.

9. Continuous Learning:

Remember that web development is a field that constantly evolves. Keep exploring new technologies, frameworks, and best practices to stay at the forefront of web development.

By diving into advanced JavaScript and frameworks, you'll be equipped to create more sophisticated and feature-rich web applications, making you a versatile and sought-after web developer in the industry.

10.2 Backend Development and Server-Side Programming

In this chapter, we'll explore the world of backend development and server-side programming. While frontend development focuses on what users see and interact with in their browsers, backend development powers the behind-the-scenes functionality of web applications. It involves handling data, processing requests, and managing the server that serves your frontend.

Why Backend Development Matters:

Backend development is crucial because it enables you to build robust, data-driven web applications with features like user authentication, database integration, and server-side logic. Let's delve into the key components and concepts of backend development:

1. Server and Routing:

  - **Web Servers:** Learn about web server technologies like Node.js, Python's Django, Ruby on Rails, or Java Spring Boot. These frameworks allow you to create server applications that can handle HTTP requests.

  - **Routing:** Explore routing mechanisms to define how your server responds to different URL paths. This is crucial for directing requests to the right parts of your application.

2. APIs and RESTful Services:

- **APIs (Application Programming Interfaces):** Understand how to design and build APIs that allow your frontend to communicate with the backend. Learn about RESTful principles for designing clean and scalable APIs.

- **Authentication and Authorization:** Implement user authentication and authorization to secure your APIs and control access to sensitive data and functionalities.

3. Databases and Data Modeling:

- **Database Management:** Explore various database systems like SQL (e.g., MySQL, PostgreSQL) and NoSQL (e.g., MongoDB) and understand how to interact with them from your server.

- **Data Modeling:** Learn the art of designing database schemas that efficiently store and retrieve data for your application's needs.

4. Middleware and Server-Side Logic:

- **Middleware:** Discover how middleware functions can process requests before they reach your application's routes. Middleware is useful for tasks like logging, authentication checks, and error handling.

- **Server-Side Logic:** Write server-side code to handle business logic, process data, and respond to client requests.

5. Performance and Scalability:

- **Caching:** Implement caching strategies to improve the performance of your backend by reducing redundant database queries.

- **Load Balancing:** Explore load balancing techniques to distribute incoming traffic across multiple servers for better scalability.

6. Server Deployment and Management:

- **Deployment:** Learn how to deploy your server application to production environments using platforms like AWS, Heroku, or Docker containers.

- **Monitoring and Troubleshooting:** Understand how to monitor server health, diagnose issues, and troubleshoot problems in a live environment.

7. Backend Frameworks:

- **Node.js:** Dive into Node.js for JavaScript-based server-side development. Node.js is known for its event-driven, non-blocking I/O model.

- **Python (Django/Flask):** Explore Python's web frameworks like Django (batteries-included) and Flask (lightweight) for backend development.

- **Ruby on Rails:** Discover Ruby on Rails, a robust and developer-friendly framework for building web applications.

   - Java (Spring Boot): Learn about Spring Boot for Java-based backend development, which emphasizes convention over configuration.

Backend development complements frontend skills, enabling you to build complete, end-to-end web applications. By mastering backend development, you'll have the tools to create interactive, data-driven, and secure web applications that can handle real-world challenges.

10.3 Database Integration

Database integration is a critical component of modern web development, allowing you to store, retrieve, and manipulate data for your web applications. In this chapter, we'll explore the various aspects of integrating databases into your web projects.

Understanding Database Integration:

Database integration involves connecting your web application to a database system, whether it's a relational database like MySQL or PostgreSQL or a NoSQL database like MongoDB. Here's what you need to know:

1. Relational vs. NoSQL Databases:

  - **Relational Databases**: Understand the concepts of tables, rows, and columns in relational databases. Learn about SQL (Structured Query Language) for querying and managing data.

  - **NoSQL Databases:** Explore the flexibility of NoSQL databases, which are suitable for unstructured or semi-structured data. Common types include document-oriented, key-value, and column-family databases.

2. Database Models and Design:

  - **Entity-Relationship Diagrams (ERD):** Use ERDs to visualize the relationships between tables and define the structure of your relational database.

- **Schema Design:** Learn about designing database schemas that efficiently represent your application's data and support complex queries.

3. Database Connectivity:

- **Database Drivers:** Depending on your programming language (e.g., Node.js, Python, Java), use appropriate database drivers or libraries to connect to the database system.

- **Connection Pooling:** Implement connection pooling to manage and reuse database connections efficiently.

4. Data Access:

- **CRUD Operations:** Master Create, Read, Update, and Delete (CRUD) operations to interact with data in the database.

- **Query Optimization:** Optimize database queries to improve performance. Learn about indexing and query planning.

5. ORM (Object-Relational Mapping):

- **ORM Libraries:** Explore ORM libraries like Sequelize (Node.js), SQLAlchemy (Python), or Hibernate (Java) to interact with databases using object-oriented models.

- **Benefits of ORM:** Understand the advantages of using ORM, such as simplifying database interactions and reducing the need for manual SQL queries.

6. NoSQL Database Integration:

- **Document Stores:** Dive into using document-oriented databases like MongoDB, where data is stored in JSON-like documents.

- **Scalability:** Learn how NoSQL databases can provide horizontal scalability for applications with high data volume and traffic.

7. Database Security:

- **Authentication:** Implement secure authentication methods for database access.

- **Authorization**: Control user permissions and access to database resources.

- **Data Encryption:** Secure sensitive data through encryption methods.

8. Handling Database Errors:

- **Error Handling:** Develop robust error-handling mechanisms to deal with database-related errors gracefully.

- **Transactions:** Learn about database transactions and how to maintain data consistency.

9. Real-world Scenarios:

- **Web Applications:** See how database integration applies to various web application scenarios, such as e-commerce, social media, and content management systems.

- **Scaling Strategies:** Explore strategies for scaling databases as your application grows.

Database integration is a fundamental skill for web developers, enabling you to build feature-rich applications that store and retrieve data efficiently and securely. Understanding both relational and NoSQL databases, along with their associated best practices, is essential for creating dynamic web experiences.

10.4 Building Web Applications

In this chapter, we'll delve into the process of building web applications, which represent the culmination of your web development skills. Building web applications involves integrating various technologies, tools, and best practices to create feature-rich, interactive, and dynamic online experiences. Let's explore the key steps and considerations for building web applications:

1. Project Planning and Architecture:

- **Project Scope:** Define the goals, features, and user requirements for your web application.

- **Architecture:** Choose an appropriate architecture pattern, such as Model-View-Controller (MVC) or Single Page Application (SPA), based on your project's needs.

2. Frontend Development:

- **User Interface (UI) Design:** Create an intuitive and visually appealing user interface using HTML, CSS, and JavaScript. Consider responsive design for mobile compatibility.

- **Client-Side Frameworks:** Explore popular frontend frameworks like React, Angular, or Vue.js for building interactive user interfaces.

- **State Management:** Implement state management solutions like Redux (for React) or Vuex (for Vue.js) to manage complex application states.

3. Backend Development:

- Server-Side Programming: Choose a backend technology stack (Node.js, Python, Ruby on Rails, etc.) to handle server-side logic and data processing.

- API Design: Design RESTful or GraphQL APIs to facilitate communication between the frontend and backend components.

- Authentication and Authorization: Implement user authentication and authorization mechanisms to secure your application.

4. Data Storage and Databases:

- Database Integration: Connect to a database system (SQL or NoSQL) to store and retrieve application data.

- ORM or ODM: Utilize Object-Relational Mapping (ORM) or Object-Document Mapping (ODM) libraries for efficient data manipulation.

- Data Validation: Implement data validation and sanitization to ensure data integrity.

5. Backend APIs and Services:

- Third-Party Integrations: Integrate third-party services, APIs, or microservices for added functionality (e.g., payment gateways, social media logins).

- **Serverless Computing:** Explore serverless platforms like AWS Lambda or Azure Functions for scalable and cost-effective backend operations.

6. Application Testing:

- **Unit and Integration Testing:** Write tests to ensure the reliability and functionality of your code.

- **User Acceptance Testing:** Involve users or stakeholders to validate that the application meets their expectations.

7. Deployment and Hosting:

- **DevOps Practices:** Implement continuous integration and continuous deployment (CI/CD) pipelines for automated testing and deployment.

- **Web Hosting:** Select a web hosting provider and configure the server environment for your application.

8. Performance Optimization:

- **Load Balancing:** Set up load balancers to distribute incoming traffic and ensure application scalability.

- **Caching:** Implement caching strategies to reduce database and server load.

9. Monitoring and Error Handling:

- **Logging:** Implement logging mechanisms to track application behavior and diagnose issues.

- **Error Handling:** Develop robust error-handling strategies to handle exceptions gracefully.

10. Security Considerations:

- **Web Application Security:** Apply security best practices to protect against common web vulnerabilities, such as Cross-Site Scripting (XSS) and SQL injection.

- **Data Encryption:** Secure sensitive data with encryption mechanisms.

11. Scalability and Future Growth:

- **Scalability Planning:** Prepare your application for future growth by designing for scalability and considering horizontal scaling options.

12. User Feedback and Iteration:

- **User Feedback:** Gather user feedback and conduct usability testing to make iterative improvements.

Building web applications is a complex yet rewarding endeavor. It requires a combination of frontend and backend development skills, along with a strong focus on user experience, security, and performance. As you work through the process of building web applications, you'll gain valuable experience and have the opportunity to create impactful digital experiences for users.

10.5 A Glimpse into the Future of Web Development

In this final chapter, we will explore emerging trends and technologies that offer a glimpse into the exciting future of web development. The field of web development is constantly evolving, and staying up-to-date with the latest advancements can give you a competitive edge. Here are some key areas to keep an eye on:

1. Progressive Web Apps (PWAs):

  - **Definition:** Progressive Web Apps are web applications that offer a native app-like experience, including offline access, push notifications, and fast loading.

  - **Why They Matter:** PWAs are gaining popularity due to their ability to provide a seamless user experience across devices and platforms.

  - **How to Implement:** Learn about service workers, manifest files, and best practices for building PWAs.

2. WebAssembly (Wasm):

  - **What Is It:** WebAssembly is a binary instruction format that enables high-performance execution of code on web browsers.

  - **Why It Matters:** WebAssembly allows developers to run code written in languages like C, C++, and Rust in web applications, opening up new possibilities for performance optimization.

  - **How to Use It:** Explore WebAssembly and consider its applications in your projects.

3. WebXR (Extended Reality):

- **Definition:** WebXR is a set of web standards that enable augmented reality (AR) and virtual reality (VR) experiences in web browsers.

- **Why It Matters:** WebXR has the potential to revolutionize industries like gaming, education, and healthcare by making immersive experiences more accessible.

- **How to Get Started:** Familiarize yourself with WebXR APIs and consider how they can be integrated into your projects.

4. Serverless Computing:

- **What Is It:** Serverless computing is an architecture where developers can run code in response to events without the need to manage server infrastructure.

- **Why It Matters:** Serverless architectures can lead to cost savings, improved scalability, and faster development cycles.

- **How to Adopt It:** Explore serverless platforms like AWS Lambda, Azure Functions, and Google Cloud Functions.

5. Artificial Intelligence (AI) and Machine Learning (ML):

- **Application Areas**: AI and ML are increasingly used in web development for tasks like chatbots, recommendation systems, and content generation.

- Why They Matter: These technologies can enhance user experiences and automate various aspects of web applications.

- Getting Started: Learn about AI/ML frameworks and tools, and consider how they can be applied to your projects.

6. Web 3.0 and Blockchain:

- Definition: Web 3.0 represents a vision of a decentralized, user-centric web, often associated with blockchain technology.

- Why It Matters: Web 3.0 has the potential to reshape how data is controlled and monetized on the internet.

- Exploring Blockchain: Understand blockchain basics and explore blockchain platforms for potential use cases.

7. Ethical and Inclusive Design:

- Importance: The future of web development also includes a strong emphasis on ethical design, accessibility, and inclusivity.

- How to Practice It: Stay informed about accessibility standards, ethical design principles, and inclusive user experiences.

As you look to the future of web development, keep in mind that adaptability and continuous learning will be your greatest assets. Embrace new technologies and methodologies as they emerge, and always prioritize creating web experiences that are user-friendly, secure, and accessible to all. The future of web development is full of exciting possibilities, and by staying informed and prepared, you can be a part of shaping it.

Appendix A
HTML and CSS Reference

A.1 HTML Elements and Attributes

In this HTML reference appendix, we will provide a comprehensive guide to HTML elements and attributes commonly used in web development. Understanding HTML is fundamental to building web pages and applications. Let's dive into the essential HTML elements and attributes:

HTML Elements:

1. `<html>`: The root element that encapsulates the entire HTML document.

2. `<head>`: Contains metadata about the document, such as the title and links to external resources.

3. `<title>`: Sets the title of the web page displayed in the browser tab.

4. `<meta>`: Provides metadata like character encoding and viewport settings.

5. `<link>`: Links external resources like stylesheets and icons.

6. `<style>`: Embeds CSS styles directly within the HTML document.

7. `<script>`: Embeds JavaScript code or links to external JavaScript files.

8. `<body>`: Contains the visible content of the web page.

9. `<header>`: Represents introductory content at the beginning of a section.

10. `<nav>`: Defines navigation links within the document.

11. `<main>`: Contains the primary content of the web page.

12. `<article>`: Represents a self-contained composition like a blog post.

13. `<section>`: Defines a thematic grouping of content within an article.

14. `<aside>`: Contains content tangentially related to the main content.

15. `<footer>`: Represents the footer section of a document or section.

16. `<div>`: A generic container for grouping and styling purposes.

Common Attributes:

1. `class`: Assigns one or more class names to an element for styling with CSS.

2. `id`: Provides a unique identifier for an element.

3. `style`: Applies inline CSS styles directly to an element.

4. `src`: Specifies the source URL for elements like images and scripts.

5. `href`: Defines the hyperlink reference for anchor (`<a>`) elements.

6. `alt`: Provides alternative text for images for accessibility.

7. `width` and `height`: Sets the dimensions of images and other elements.

8. `target`: Specifies where to open linked documents (e.g., in a new tab).

9. `rel`: Defines the relationship between the current document and linked resources.

10. `aria-*`: ARIA attributes for enhancing accessibility.

11. `data-*`: Custom data attributes for storing extra information.

In this reference, we will detail the usage, syntax, and examples of these HTML elements and attributes. Understanding how to use these fundamental building blocks is crucial for creating well-structured and accessible web pages.

By the end of this section, you will have a solid grasp of HTML's core elements and attributes, empowering you to create web content that is both functional and visually appealing.

Let's begin exploring HTML elements and attributes in more depth.

A.2 Common CSS Properties and Values

In this CSS reference appendix, we will provide an extensive guide to common CSS (Cascading Style Sheets) properties and values. CSS is crucial for styling and designing web pages. Let's delve into some of the most frequently used CSS properties and their values:

Common CSS Properties:

1. `color`: Sets the text color.

2. `font-family`: Specifies the font for text.

3. `font-size`: Determines the size of text.

4. `font-weight`: Defines the thickness of text characters.

5. `text-align`: Aligns text horizontally (left, center, right).

6. `text-decoration`: Adds decorations to text (underline, overline, line-through).

7. `background-color`: Sets the background color of elements.

8. `margin`: Controls the spacing around elements.

9. `padding`: Manages the spacing within elements.

10. `border`: Styles and adds borders to elements.

11. `width` and `height`: Sets the dimensions of elements.

12. `display`: Specifies how elements are rendered (block, inline, inline-block).

13. `position`: Determines the positioning method of elements (relative, absolute, fixed).

14. `float`: Floats elements to the left or right.

15. `clear`: Clears floated elements.

16. `border-radius`: Rounds the corners of elements.

17. `box-shadow`: Adds shadows to elements.

18. `text-transform`: Modifies the capitalization of text (uppercase, lowercase, capitalize).

19. `line-height`: Sets the height of lines within text.

20. `z-index`: Controls the stacking order of elements.

Common CSS Values:

1. Color Values: Hexadecimal (`#RRGGBB`), RGB (`rgb(0, 0, 255)`), named colors (`red`), and more.

2. Length Values: Pixels (`px`), percentages (`%`), em units (`em`), and more.

3. Font Values: Font names, font size values (`12px`, `1.2em`), and generic font families (`sans-serif`).

4. Text Values: `left`, `center`, `right`, `justify`, `underline`, `overline`, `line-through`, etc.

5. Display Values: `block`, `inline`, `inline-block`, `none`, and more.

6. Position Values: `static`, `relative`, `absolute`, `fixed`, and `sticky`.

7. Border Values: Border width, style, and color (`1px solid black`).

8. Background Values: Background color, image, position, and repeat.

9. Box Model Values: Margin, padding, and border values.

10. Gradient Values: Linear and radial gradients.

11. Animation Values: Keyframes, animation duration, timing function, etc.

Throughout this reference, we will provide detailed explanations, examples, and use cases for each CSS property and value. Understanding how to apply CSS is essential for creating visually appealing and responsive web layouts.

By the end of this section, you will have a solid grasp of common CSS properties and values, empowering you to style web content effectively.

Let's begin exploring common CSS properties and values in more detail.

Appendix B
JavaScript Reference

B.1 JavaScript Objects and Methods

In this JavaScript reference, we will explore essential JavaScript objects and methods that are fundamental to web development. JavaScript is a versatile programming language that enables dynamic and interactive web experiences. Understanding these core objects and methods is key to becoming proficient in JavaScript.

Common JavaScript Objects:

1. `String`: Represents text and provides methods for manipulating text strings.

2. `Number`: Represents numeric values and offers methods for mathematical operations.

3. `Array`: Stores collections of data and provides methods for working with arrays.

4. `Object`: A versatile data structure used to store key-value pairs.

5. `Date`: Represents dates and times, allowing you to work with dates and perform date calculations.

6. `Math`: Provides mathematical constants and functions for advanced calculations.

7. `RegExp`: Enables the creation and manipulation of regular expressions for pattern matching.

8. `Function`: Defines functions and methods, allowing you to create reusable code blocks.

Common JavaScript Methods:

1. `parseInt()` and `parseFloat()`: Converts strings to integers or floating-point numbers.

2. `toString()`: Converts data to a string representation.

3. `toFixed()` and `toPrecision()`: Formats numbers with a specific number of decimal places.

4. `split()`: Splits a string into an array of substrings based on a delimiter.

5. `join()`: Combines array elements into a single string using a separator.

6. `push()` and `pop()`: Add or remove elements from the end of an array.

7. `shift()` and `unshift()`: Add or remove elements from the beginning of an array.

8. `Object.keys()` and `Object.values()`: Retrieve keys or values from an object.

9. `Date` methods like `getFullYear()`, `getMonth()`, and `getDate()`: Extract date components.

10. `Math` methods like `round()`, `ceil()`, and `floor()`: Perform mathematical operations.

Throughout this reference, we will provide detailed explanations, examples, and use cases for each JavaScript object and method. Understanding how to work with these fundamental components is essential for JavaScript programming.

By the end of this section, you will have a solid understanding of JavaScript's core objects and methods, allowing you to build interactive and dynamic web applications.

Let's begin exploring JavaScript objects and methods in more detail.

B.2 Common JavaScript Events

In this JavaScript reference, we'll delve into common JavaScript events that play a pivotal role in creating dynamic and interactive web applications. Events are actions or occurrences that happen in the browser, such as user interactions or changes in the document's state. JavaScript allows you to listen for and respond to these events, enabling you to build responsive and engaging web experiences.

Common JavaScript Events:

1. Click Event: Triggered when an element is clicked, typically used for handling user interactions like button clicks and link navigation.

```javascript
element.addEventListener('click', function() {
  // Your code here
});
```

2. Mouseover and Mouseout Events: Fired when the mouse pointer enters or leaves an element, useful for creating hover effects.

```javascript
element.addEventListener('mouseover', function() {
  // Mouse enters the element
});
```

```javascript
element.addEventListener('mouseout', function() {

  // Mouse leaves the element

});
```

3. Keydown and Keyup Events: Capture keyboard input events, such as when a key is pressed or released.

```javascript
document.addEventListener('keydown', function(event) {

  // Key is pressed

});

document.addEventListener('keyup', function(event) {

  // Key is released

});
```

4. Submit Event: Occurs when a form is submitted, allowing you to handle form data before it's sent to the server.

```javascript
form.addEventListener('submit', function(event) {
```

```javascript
event.preventDefault(); // Prevents the form from actually submitting

// Your form handling code here

});
```

5. Change Event: Fired when the value of an input element changes, such as when selecting an option in a dropdown.

```javascript
input.addEventListener('change', function() {

// Input value changed

});
```

6. Load and Unload Events: Triggered when a page finishes loading or unloading, useful for executing actions when the page is ready or before it's closed.

```javascript
window.addEventListener('load', function() {

// Page is fully loaded

});

window.addEventListener('unload', function() {

// Page is being unloaded (e.g., when navigating to another page)
```

```
});
```

7. Resize Event: Occurs when the browser window is resized, allowing you to adjust your layout dynamically.

```javascript
window.addEventListener('resize', function() {
  // Window size changed
});
```

8. Custom Events: You can also create and dispatch custom events to communicate between different parts of your application.

```javascript
const customEvent = new Event('custom');
element.dispatchEvent(customEvent);
```

Throughout this reference, we'll provide detailed explanations, examples, and best practices for working with these common JavaScript events. Understanding how to use events effectively is essential for creating dynamic and responsive web applications.

By the end of this section, you'll have a solid understanding of how to work with events in JavaScript and how to make your web applications interactive and engaging. Let's dive into the world of JavaScript events.

Glossary

Key Terms and Definitions

In this glossary, we'll provide concise and clear explanations for key terms and definitions commonly used in the field of web development. Understanding these terms is essential for anyone venturing into web development, whether you're a beginner or an experienced developer looking to refresh your knowledge. Let's dive into the world of web development terminology.

1. HTML (Hypertext Markup Language): HTML is the standard markup language used to create web pages. It structures content on the web, using elements like headings, paragraphs, and links.

2. CSS (Cascading Style Sheets): CSS is a stylesheet language that describes the presentation of HTML documents. It controls how elements are styled, such as their layout, colors, and fonts.

3. JavaScript: JavaScript is a programming language that enables interactivity and dynamic behavior in web pages. It's commonly used for tasks like form validation, animations, and manipulating the DOM.

4. DOM (Document Object Model): The DOM is a programming interface for web documents. It represents the page so that programs can change the document structure, style, and content dynamically.

5. HTTP (Hypertext Transfer Protocol): HTTP is the protocol used for transferring data over the web. It defines how messages are formatted and transmitted between the client (usually a web browser) and the server.

6. HTTPS (Hypertext Transfer Protocol Secure): HTTPS is a secure version of HTTP. It encrypts data sent between the client and server, enhancing security and privacy.

7. URL (Uniform Resource Locator): A URL is a web address used to specify the location of a resource on the internet. It includes the protocol (e.g., http:// or https://), domain, and path.

8. API (Application Programming Interface): An API defines a set of rules and protocols for building and interacting with software applications. Web APIs allow different web services to communicate.

9. Responsive Design: Responsive design is an approach to web design that ensures a web page's layout and content adapt to various screen sizes and devices, providing an optimal user experience.

10. Frontend Development: Frontend development involves creating the user interface and user experience of a website or web application. It typically focuses on HTML, CSS, and JavaScript.

11. Backend Development: Backend development involves building the server-side of web applications. It includes server configuration, databases, and handling server requests.

12. Database: A database is a structured collection of data. In web development, databases store information that can be retrieved, manipulated, and displayed on web pages.

13. Framework: A framework is a pre-built set of tools and conventions that speeds up web development. Popular web frameworks include React, Angular, and Vue.js.

14. SEO (Search Engine Optimization): SEO is the practice of optimizing a website to improve its visibility in search engine results, increasing organic (non-paid) traffic.

15. Web Hosting: Web hosting is the service of storing and making web content accessible on the internet. Web hosting providers offer server space and resources for websites.

16. Cookies: Cookies are small pieces of data stored on a user's device. They are often used for tracking and authentication purposes on websites.

17. Responsive Images: Responsive images adapt to different screen sizes and resolutions, helping to optimize page load times and user experience.

18. Version Control: Version control systems, like Git, track changes to code, allowing multiple developers to collaborate, revert changes, and manage project history.

19. CMS (Content Management System): A CMS is a software platform that simplifies website creation and management, often used for blogs and content-heavy sites.

20. API Endpoint: An API endpoint is a specific URL or URI used to access a web service or API. It defines the location and behavior of a particular resource.

This glossary serves as a valuable reference for understanding the terminology and concepts you'll encounter in the world of web development. Whether you're reading documentation, collaborating with other developers, or building your own projects, having a solid grasp of these terms will empower you to excel in the field.

Conclusion

In the ever-evolving landscape of web development, this comprehensive guide has aimed to provide you with a solid foundation, practical skills, and valuable insights into the world of creating websites and web applications. Whether you're a beginner taking your first steps into web development or an experienced developer looking to broaden your knowledge, we hope this journey has been enriching and rewarding.

Throughout this guide, we've explored the core technologies that power the web, including HTML, CSS, and JavaScript. We've delved into responsive web design, providing the tools and techniques needed to craft websites that look great and function seamlessly on a variety of devices. You've also learned about web development best practices, security, and accessibility, ensuring that your creations are both user-friendly and secure.

We've covered projects ranging from personal portfolio websites to interactive photo galleries and contact forms with server-side integration. These hands-on projects have allowed you to apply what you've learned and gain practical experience, helping you become a more proficient web developer.

Furthermore, we've touched on the future of web development, introducing advanced topics like JavaScript frameworks, backend development, and database integration, opening the door to endless possibilities in web application development.

As you continue your web development journey, remember that the web is a dynamic and ever-changing environment. Stay curious, keep exploring, and remain adaptable to new technologies and trends. The web development community is a vibrant one, and there are countless resources and opportunities for learning and growth.

We would like to express our sincere gratitude to you, our reader, for embarking on this learning journey with us. Your dedication and curiosity are what drive innovation and progress in the field of web development. We hope that this guide has been a valuable resource, and we encourage you to continue exploring, building, and sharing your creations with the world.

Thank you for choosing this guide, and we wish you the very best in your web development endeavors. May your passion for coding and your love for the web lead you to great success and fulfillment in this exciting field.

Happy coding, and keep building amazing things for the web!

www.ingramcontent.com/pod-product-compliance
Lightning Source LLC
Chambersburg PA
CBHW060550060326
40690CB00017B/3664